RUDOLPH *the red-nosed reindeer*

Ronald D. Lankford, Jr.

RUDOLPH

the
RED-NOSED
REINDEER

An American Hero

ForeEdge

ForeEdge

An imprint of University Press of New England

www.upne.com

© 2017 Ronald D. Lankford, Jr.

All rights reserved

Manufactured in the United States of America

Designed by Mindy Basinger Hill

Typeset in Garamond Premier Pro

For permission to reproduce any of the material
in this book, contact Permissions, University Press
of New England, One Court Street, Suite 250,
Lebanon NH 03766; or visit www.upne.com

Paperback ISBN: 978-1-61168-735-4

Ebook ISBN: 978-1-61168-975-4

Library of Congress Cataloging-in-Publication data
available on request.

5   4   3   2   1

To Elizabeth C. S. Lankford

contents

acknowledgments

First I would like to thank my wife, Elizabeth Lankford, who has always been my first reader. She remained enthusiastic about Rudolph, even while living with year-round Christmas for the duration of this project. I also appreciated my correspondence with author Tim Hollis. Tim kindly shared his own knowledge of Rudolph while providing several key pieces of research.

A number of people at college and public libraries also aided my research: Peter Carini and Joshua Shaw at the Rauner Library at Dartmouth; Stephanie Hunter and Winston Barham at the University of Virginia Music Library; Belinda Carroll at the Knight-Capron Library at Lynchburg College; Jeannie Isaacs at the Campbell County Library in Rustburg, Virginia; Lesley Martin at the Chicago History Museum; Amanda Stow and John R. Waggener at the American Heritage Center; Elizabeth Dunn at Duke University; Janet C. Olsen at Northeastern University Library; and George Willeman with the Library of Congress. For everyone else I corresponded with and for those who generously provided images for the project, thank you.

I would like to thank both Bronwyn Becker at the University Press of New England and Glenn Novak. I would also like to thank my agent, Robert Lecker, for his help with developing and finally placing this book project.

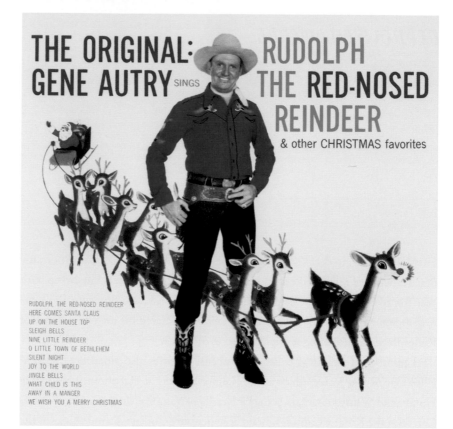

Gene Autry, *Rudolph the Red-Nosed Reindeer*, 33⅓ album (Challenge, 1957)

introduction
RESEARCHING RUDOLPH

As a kid I remember listening to Gene Autry sing "Rudolph the Red-Nosed Reindeer" dozens of times each Christmas. It was the late 1960s, and I lived with my parents and a younger brother and sister in Norfolk, Virginia. Christmas was a big deal. We helped Mom decorate the tree, with reflectors behind those big, primary-colored bulbs. She never let us touch the tinsel, since we—the kids—tended to throw it in clumps on the white pine. There were also cherry cookies and Christmas spice cake. Dad decorated the picture window in the living room, drawing Christmas scenes with white shoe polish, and drew a smaller scene on the bathroom mirror. And in the background, through whatever we were doing, Christmas songs and carols—the Lennon Sisters, Johnny Mathis, and Chet Atkins—always played. Rudolph, though, was the best. Without him, I believe, Christmas would never have been complete.

The Autry album we played was called *Rudolph the Red-Nosed Reindeer* and had been issued by Autry's very own label, Challenge, in 1957. This was back when marketing folks went to a lot of trouble to create an arresting image for a 33⅓ album cover. I was fascinated by the picture of Autry, dressed as a giant cowboy, with Santa's sleigh and the reindeer team flying underneath his legs. This "Rudolph" was not the original: the original song had been recorded by Autry for Columbia in 1949. But it was the only version we knew, and the album had the added bonus of a second Rudolph song, "Nine Little Reindeer." My brother and I preferred the first side of *Rudolph the Red-Nosed Reindeer* with all the Santa and Rudolph songs, as opposed to the carols on side two.

What strikes me now is how much we accepted Rudolph as a part of our traditional family Christmas. Rudolph seemed, in song (1949), in the Little Golden Books version of Robert L. May's story (1958), and in the Rankin/Bass animated TV special (1964), as much a part of our Christmas celebration as Santa Claus and all the lore—the elves, the North Pole, Mrs. Claus, and the other eight reindeer—that went with him. Santa Claus, however, could be traced back in a somewhat recognizable form for a hundred years. Rudolph, a sacred part of our family's holiday tradition, could be traced only to 1939. From the standpoint of 1969, Rudolph could hardly qualify as a central myth of an American Christmas, but we did not know that. Likewise, while Rudolph could hardly qualify as genuine folk culture, we—along with millions of others—accepted him as such.

I never planned to write a book about Rudolph. He was so much a part of my childhood, so much a part of the kind of Christmas I had grown up with, that I just accepted him as having always been there. It did not occur to me that Rudolph—the modest hero with a secret resource—reflected deeply held American values.

My innocence about the connection between Rudolph and our holiday values started to change a couple of years ago when I was writing about American Christmas songs. One of those songs, naturally, was Johnny Marks's "Rudolph the Red-Nosed Reindeer." As I began researching, several things occupied my thoughts. Rudolph, as James H. Barnett noted in 1954, was the only new addition to our Christmas lore in a hundred years. While Barnett wrote this in the 1950s, it remains true: as much as we love Frosty and other Christmas critters, none of them have become as central as Rudolph. The truth of this, though, fails to explain why Rudolph was accepted into Christmas lore so quickly. Likewise, it fails to explain how Rudolph's image has remained expansive enough to speak to Americans across—as I write this—seven decades.

The origin of Rudolph the Red-Nosed Reindeer also fascinated me. Many people, listening to the song or watching the 1964 cartoon, had completely forgotten

Rudolph's origins as a promotion in 1939 and 1946 for Montgomery Ward. Unlike Santa Claus, Rudolph had no European folk myths to draw from. Instead, he was born in the imagination of copywriter Robert L. May, who was employed by Montgomery Ward. The idea was simply to give away thousands and thousands of copies of *Rudolph*, in booklet form, at Ward's six-hundred-plus stores to children accompanied by a parent, drawing the family into the department store for the all-important holiday season. Merchandise, the same kind that accompanies any Disney movie promotion today, would follow.

Despite these commercial origins, children and even parents accepted Rudolph as though he were the genuine article. Folklorists could label the Jolly Green Giant "fakelore" or use the term "industrial folklore" to define the Trix rabbit, but children—learning about the reindeer in books, View-Master reels, a game, a cartoon, in song, and multiple pieces of merchandise—seemed oblivious to academic concerns. Clearly, Robert L. May wrote *Rudolph* in 1939; equally clear, he wrote *Rudolph* at the request of his supervisor as a work-for-hire at Montgomery Ward. Likewise, a popular groundswell greeted Rudolph on his introduction in 1939 and reintroduction in 1946; this groundswell was heightened considerably, however, by Montgomery Ward's giveaway of six million copies of the *Rudolph* booklet. While we can argue whether commercial or creative forces exerted more influence over Rudolph's growth in popular culture, both had a role to play. Rudolph's grounding in both commercial and folk culture produced, I believe, an intriguing paradox worth looking into.

I also realized that it would be a paradox that was sometimes difficult to view in full. Often, I believe, our commercial culture seems invisible to us. We love stories about creators (Robert May) who grew wealthy (Johnny Marks), fulfilling the American dream: these individuals tell us that our success myth is real. The partners behind the scenes (Montgomery Ward, Columbia Records) remain either imperceptible or are understood as benign. We learn that Ward's generously returned Rudolph's copyright to May in 1947 and that GE's sponsorship allowed Rankin/Bass the freedom to create the animated *Rudolph* in 1964. For Ward's and GE, however, these sponsorships were considered investments against future profits. To call attention to the nuts and bolts of this sponsorship is less a criticism than an attempt to balance our understanding of how Rudolph became Rudolph.

One other thing stood out to me. If the story of Rudolph himself seemed to represent certain ideas about American culture—the modest hero with a strong strain of individualism—the stories surrounding Rudolph, his creation and development, were more difficult to decipher. It became evident to me, even before starting this project, that many of the stories about Rudolph contained contradictions, along with story arcs that were too perfect. The stories about the creation of Rudolph, then, had become as encased in myth as Rudolph himself.

May, with the help of journalists, emphasized different details when speaking of Rudolph at different points of his life. For instance, one story repeated that Rudolph had been written to comfort his four-year-old daughter whose mother was dying of cancer; another, that Rudolph was basically a Montgomery Ward assignment. What was the truth? And how could I separate these (and many other) stories—pointing out false information—without stepping on somebody's toes? All of this, of course, would be greatly complicated by the seventy-five years that separated me from Rudolph's birth.

I did know, from the outset, that one person stood at the center of the Rudolph story: Robert L. May. Yes, there would be other important players—cartoonist Max Fleischer, songwriter Johnny Marks, singer Gene Autry, and animators Rankin/Bass. But without May, there would have been no Montgomery Ward promotion of Rudolph in 1939, no cartoon by Fleischer in 1948, no song by Marks in 1949, and no Rankin/Bass special in 1964. It was May's basic vision—the vision of a young, misunderstood reindeer with an untapped talent—that remained at the center of every Rudolph story line. If I wanted to make this book work, I would have find out more about May.

RUDOLPH *the red-nosed reindeer*

one

ROBERT L. MAY, MONTGOMERY WARD, AND A REINDEER NAMED RUDOLPH

As with Mickey Mouse (1928), Superman (1938), and many other popular cultural characters, Rudolph the Red-Nosed Reindeer had a proud parent: Robert Lewis May. May was born on July 27, 1905, in New Rochelle, New York, and many of his early experiences would give shape to Rudolph. As the title of a self-penned article later explained, "Rudolph and I were something alike."[1]

One writer has described May as growing up in a middle-class household in New Rochelle, with a brother, Richard, and two sisters, Evelyn and Margaret. Margaret May later married Johnny Marks, who would condense May's *Rudolph* story into song. May's father, Milton, operated a lumber business, the May Lumber Company, though the family would fall on hard times during the Depression.[2]

May has been described by family and himself as frail, small, and "poorly coordinated."[3] "My dad had been kind of a runt," Barbara Lewis, May's oldest daughter, later told a newspaper. "He was ahead of [his] age group in school and he wasn't athletic. He was teased. He knew what it was like to be the underdog."[4] May, smaller than most of his classmates, had skipped one or two grades.[5]

After attending New Rochelle High School for four years, May attended Dartmouth College in Hanover, New Hampshire, in the early 1920s (probably starting in 1922). He majored in psychology and took classes in German, philosophy, French, English, Latin, zoology, and evolution.[6] May was an honor student, a member of Alpha Sigma Phi, and graduated Phi Beta Kappa in 1926.

Following college, May took a series of jobs in advertising and sales, moving to new locations and new positions frequently. Between 1926 and 1931, he worked as a copywriter for R. H. Macy and Co. and as an advertising manager for J. L. Brandeis, Rich's, and Butterick Co. On November 29, 1928, in Chicago, he married Evelyn Heymann, who had attended Radcliffe. In 1932 May went to work at Gimbels in New York as an advertising copywriter, a position he would keep for the next four years.[7]

Often noted for his quiet nature, May also exuded the easy warmth that comes through in his written letters. This warmth was often accompanied with humor. One early chronicler, speaking with May after the initial publication of *Rudolph*, began his description of the copywriter as "slight and dark": "He looks very much like a serious student and has a Phi Beta Kappa key to prove that he is. On the other hand, upon the slightest provocation his eyes may begin to twinkle and with but a slight, shy smile he twists words into a hilarity-provoking bit of wit."[8] In 1935, while still working for Gimbels in New York City, May wrote a short note to the editor of the *Dartmouth Alumni Magazine* announcing the birth of his and Evelyn's daughter Barbara:

> Away back in December, your secretary must have spotted in your mail pile a typewritten Gimbel envelope addressed to you. "Aha. Trying to sell something to the boss!" she probably exclaimed. "I'll fool 'em! It's probably lousy, anyway!" And the letter forthwith found the trash-basket. Which helps explain why department stores use so little direct mail advertising. . . .
>
> This time, as you see, I've fooled your guardian by using a plain envelope, and a scrawl that couldn't belong to anyone but a Dartmouth '26er. All this strategy merely to tell you that Barbara May was born on December 2. Six and one-half pounds, and so far has proved a good investment; doubled in just 2½ months!
>
> Otherwise, nothing new. Still telling the truth, more or less, for Gimbel's.[9]

In just a few years, Barbara Ruth May would help test drive her father's *Rudolph* manuscript.

Within the next ten months May accepted a new position with Montgomery Ward in Chicago. Writing to the *Dartmouth Alumni Magazine* in 1936, he reported, "Just a line to let you know I'm leaving Gimbels Saturday to join Montgomery Ward in Chicago as one of their Retail Sales Supervisors. My boss went out there in September and offered me a chance too good to pass up . . . despite the difficulty of the move. I'll stay at the Lake Shore Athletic Club for a month, then bring the family out and move 'for keeps.'"[10] It was at Montgomery Ward that May's life would take a major turn.

While May would spend much of his life working as a copywriter at Ward's, he later suggested that he had really wanted to write fiction. "Instead of writing the great American novel, as I'd once hoped, I was describing men's white shirts."[11] An interviewer noted in 1939, "Words are May's stock in trade, and people who work with him and know him will tell you only too willingly how clever he is in the use of words, not only a humorous use, but in making them express sympathy, pathos, admiration, as well as 'darn good advertising.'"[12] In 1941, when May had already written *Rudolph* but the story's future (with the approach of World War II) must have been very much in doubt, May received an honorary membership in the National Association of Authors and Journalists (for making "an outstanding contribution to contemporary literature"[13]). While May would never write the great American novel, many believed that what he did write—*Rudolph the Red-Nosed Reindeer*—was just as important.

Tracing Rudolph's Origins

Tracing Rudolph's origins has been made difficult by a simple fact: *Rudolph the Red-Nosed Reindeer* was written seventy-five years ago. Most of the people who were involved—primarily Robert L. May but also a number of other employees at Montgomery Ward—are no longer living. Even Montgomery Ward, once one of the most powerful retail giants in the United States, filed Chapter 11 in 1997 and finally closed its doors in 2000. What we know about Rudolph's origins, then, has to be pieced together from newspaper articles, interviews, and letters written earlier. Certain gaps, in a number of cases, are impossible to close.

May himself told the story of Rudolph's origins for over thirty years, sometimes emphasizing one set of details, sometimes another. Newspaper and magazine writers frequently relied on previous articles or used artistic license to make the arc of the Rudolph story more pleasing to the everyday reader. Undoubtedly a number of items—Rudolph as a purely commercial product, copyright lawsuits, and internal squabbles (at Ward's, for instance)—were never mentioned or got brushed under the editorial rug. As a result, there is not one origin story for Rudolph but two, overlapping and contradicting each other at various points.

This inexactness may seem unusual but is actually quite common, even when looking at a well-known Christmas poem like "A Visit from St. Nicholas." While the general population believes that Clement Clarke Moore wrote "A Visit from St. Nicholas" (which May used as his blueprint for creating *Rudolph*) in 1823, he was slow to claim authorship. Professor Donald Foster has used handwriting analysis to suggest that Moore could not have written the poem and that it was actually written by Henry Livingston Jr.

To complicate this kind of inexactness, folk stories often grow up around popular poems and songs. A story appeared in a newspaper in the 1940s claiming that James Lord Pierpont had written "Jingle Bells" when he was eighteen, at Mary Waterman's boardinghouse in Medford, Massachusetts. The story was told by Stella Howe, a distant relative of Waterman's, but was complicated by time: the article first appeared in the *Boston Globe* in December 1946, over one hundred years after the fact.[14] As such, the story about the origins of "Jingle Bells" was impossible to prove or disprove.

Rudolph's story of origin would spawn its own folklore. Was Rudolph written by Robert L. May to comfort his four-year-old daughter whose mother was dying of cancer? Or was Rudolph simply another assignment for a Montgomery Ward copywriter? Seventy-five years later, both stories continue to circulate.

Because these folk stories and variations reappear throughout Rudolph's life span, it's reasonable to ask how one decides which is closest to the truth; how does an author or reader weigh Rudolph folklore? In most cases, there are no exact answers. All an author can do is lay out the various accounts, making clear the strength (or lack thereof) of the sources, and offer an interpretation. The reader, meanwhile, may draw another conclusion.

Rudolph That Amazing Reindeer

One popular version of Rudolph's origin emerged in print in December 1948 in *Coronet* magazine, nine years after May had written the children's book. According to the *Coronet* article, May creates the story of Rudolph to comfort his four-year-old daughter because her mother is dying of cancer; only later, by a stroke of fate, does the story come to the attention of May's boss at Montgomery Ward, who arranges to use the story for a store-wide, holiday promotion. The *Coronet* article, "Rudolph That Amazing Reindeer," was attributed to Ralph H. Major Jr. and Stanley Frankel, although Frankel seems to have been the primary author. The article would be reprinted with slight variations in *Good Housekeeping* in December 1989 (for Rudolph's fiftieth anniversary), and versions of the story have continued to resurface on the Internet and in books such as Ace Collins's *Stories behind the Best-Loved Songs of Christmas* (2001).

As early as October 1947, Frankel had contacted *Coronet* with the idea for a story on May and Rudolph. He wrote,

> Bob May, the originator of Rudolf the Reindeer . . . is a friend of mine.
>
> He has a fabulous story to tell—how he conceived the idea at a Xmas party—how it lay around for almost ten years—and how suddenly, from unexpected sources, it will now be published in book form, put on the radio, shown in the movies, played with in games, and petted in toys—well—it would make a terrific picture story for Coronet.[15]

It would take more than a year for Frankel's story to come to fruition and would include, in the process, an interview with May (the interview does not seem to have survived). May himself mentioned the article in a letter to the *Dartmouth Alumni Magazine*: "Two weeks ago I was called down to the offices of Coronet Magazine for a lengthy interview . . . with the result that Rudolph and his old man will be the subject of a feature article in their December issue, on the newsstands November 24."[16]

The article begins by returning to May and his four-year-old daughter in the family's Chicago apartment in the winter of 1938:

> On a December night in Chicago ten years ago, a little girl climbed onto her father's lap and asked a question. It was a simple question, asked in childish curiosity, yet it had a heart-rending effect on Robert May.
>
> "Daddy," four-year-old Barbara May asked, "why isn't my Mommy just like everybody else's mommy?"[17]

May's wife, Evelyn, had been suffering from cancer for the last two years. Frankel continued: "The terrible ordeal already had shattered two adult lives. Now, May suddenly realized, the happiness of his growing daughter was also in jeopardy."[18] Barbara's question, asked in the midst of the December holiday season, demanded an answer.

Frankel sketches May's family predicament against the backdrop of dire financial circumstances. In 1938 the Depression remained an economic reality for many Americans. For the May family, doctor's visits and medicine for Evelyn stretched an already thin budget, putting the family into debt. The Mays' living space is described as a "shabby two-room apartment,"[19] the kind of place a Montgomery Ward copywriter might inhabit. Clearly Robert May, the skinny, picked-on underdog since early childhood, had missed the opportunities of his Dartmouth colleagues. "Now, at 33, May was deep in debt, depressed and miserable."[20]

May's salvation, however, lay close at hand. To answer Barbara's question he would create a children's story drawn from the emotional tumult of his own childhood: the story of a young reindeer named Rudolph who had a shiny red nose. Each night, Barbara would ask her father to recite the adventures of Rudolph one more time. Finally, May decided to prepare a rudimentary copy of the book for

"The Day Before Christmas"
or
"Rudolph, the Red-Nosed Reindeer"

'Twas the day before Christmas, and all thru the hills
The reindeer were playing... enjoying the spills

Of skating and coasting and climbing the willows
And hop-scotch and leap-frog (protected by pillows!)

While every so often they'd stop to call names
At one little deer not allowed in their games:—

"Ha ha! look at Rudolph! His nose is a sight!"
"It's red as a beet!" "Twice as big!" "Twice as bright!"

While Rudolph just wept. What else could he do?
He knew that the things they were saying were true!

Where most reindeer's noses are brown and tiny,
Poor Rudolph's was red, very large, and quite shiny.

In daylight it dazzled. (The pictures show that!)
At nighttime it glowed, like the eyes of a cat.

And rubbing dirt on it just made it look muddy.
He was mad when they nick-named him Ruddy!

Although he was lonesome, he always was good,
Obeying his parents, as good reindeer should!

But perhaps on this day Rudolph almost felt playful:—
He hoped Santa soon driving his sleighful

Of presents and candy and dollies and toys
For good little animals, good girls and boys)

He'd just as much... and this is what pleased him...
As the happier, handsomer reindeer who teased him.

All right, and a fog like the world had like a hood
He went to bed hopeful; he knew he'd been good!

✗ ✗ ✗ ✗ ✗ ✗ ✗

Handwritten draft, *Rudolph the Red Nosed Reindeer*, circa 1939 | Papers of Robert L. May, Rauner Special Collections Library, Dartmouth College; courtesy of Dartmouth College Library

her as a Christmas gift, writing the poem in verse and mimicking "A Visit from St. Nicholas." Pouring himself into the project, he wanted to provide a worthy gift for Barbara, despite the family's meager finances. As he prepared the booklet, however, tragedy struck: Evelyn died. Instead of setting the project aside during this period of grief, however, May continued to work on the booklet, determined to finish it by Christmastime.

At this nadir, with May left alone to raise his young daughter, fate intervened. He was invited to an office Christmas party at Montgomery Ward, and while he wanted to stay at home, colleagues persuaded him to attend. He brought along Barbara's gift and read it to his office-mates that evening. At first they laughed along with Rudolph's antics—May's poem seemed like no more than another part of the evening's fun and games. But as May continued, the crowd settled down and listened quietly. When he reached the end, everyone broke into applause. After several executives requested copies of *Rudolph*, the young reindeer and May's future was set on a new course. The following year, 1939, *Rudolph* would become a major promotion, with Montgomery Ward giving away 2.4 million copies for free. In 1946 after World War II, Ward's gave away another 3.6 million copies.

Rudolph's massive success through 1946, however, did little to alleviate May's financial plight: the rights to the book belonged to Montgomery Ward, not May. Still, *Rudolph's* success changed May in a fundamental way. He moved forward with his life, spending time with friends and eventually meeting Virginia Newton, a secretary at Ward's. May and Newton married in 1941 and had three children together: Joanna, Christopher, and Ginger. After the war, even May's finances began to turn around. At the end of 1946, Sewell Avery—Montgomery Ward's chief executive—released the copyright of *Rudolph* to May. "Touched by the beauty and simplicity of the Rudolph story, he ordered the copyright turned over to Bob—so that May could receive all royalties."[21]

Developing Rudolph as a new business, May soon oversaw a small empire of books, a recording, an animated cartoon, and a product line. Frankel concludes: "His fortune has now been made, and the years ahead look even brighter. Today, Bob is still a shy, thin, affable man who wants more than anything else to build security for himself and his family. He still works at Ward's—now as retail copy chief—and tackles the job with the same perseverance which has characterized his whole life."[22] May had found the balance and serenity that had eluded him during the Depression years and throughout his first wife's illness. He was living the American dream, and it had all started with a simple question asked by four-year-old girl. This portrait of May—the birth of Rudolph, the kindness of Montgomery Ward, and May's financial success—would be told over and over in the ensuing years.

Later, small details would be added to Frankel's narrative. *Good Housekeeping* published the article under Frankel's name but changed a number of words and sentences. It appears that *Good Housekeeping*, while approving of the basic content, wanted to update the style for 1989. *Good Housekeeping* also seemed to accept the facts of the original article without question. In *Stories behind the Best-Loved Songs of Christmas*, Ace Collins added that May sold the original poem to Montgomery Ward. "For a modest sum, Stewell [*sic*] Avery, the chairman of the board of Montgomery Wards, bought all rights from the cash-strapped and debt-ridden May."[23] This tidbit segued well with the original story.

The *Coronet* article provided Rudolph with a genuine folk origin and a captivating story line: The Mays become a mythical American family, struggling against the twin hardships of the Depression and illness. With a lack of prospects and little money for a better future, Robert L. May remains committed to his wife and young daughter. And even in the depths of these bleak days, he is inspired to tell a story that offers hope for the future: the ugly duckling sometimes becomes a beautiful swan. Told out of love with no thought of personal gain, *Rudolph* finds its way into the wider world, bringing the Mays fame and fortune. Rudolph's story, written for one little girl, now appeals to boys and girls everywhere.

As attractive as the *Coronet* story may be, there were a number of problems with the narrative. While many of the story's elements are accurate—Evelyn's illness, Barbara's age, and May's job as a copywriter—much of the basic premise seems to be untrue. *Rudolph the Red-Nosed Reindeer* was not written in 1938 or read by May to his colleagues at a Montgomery Ward Christmas party; neither does it seem likely that he sold "Rudolph" to the company for a "modest sum" (he may have received a bonus for his work on *Rudolph* in 1939). The *Coronet* article also leaves the impression that Evelyn May died in the winter of 1938, just as May was preparing *Rudolph* as a Christmas gift for Barbara. Evelyn May, however, died in July 1939. Frankel's story was probably the origin of all the softer versions that would follow. Interestingly, elements of the *Coronet* story were even contradicted by quotations from May that appeared, simultaneously, in a *Christian Science Monitor* article.

How Rudolph Came to Christmas

May later took the opportunity—at least twice—to provide a more accurate version of Rudolph's birth and early history. In the *Spartanburg (S.C.) Herald-Journal* of December 22, 1963, May told Rudolph's story to Alfred Balk. In 1975, a year before his death, May published a self-penned article in *Guideposts*, also offering details on Rudolph's origin. Both stories revisited older elements and added new ones while inadvertently revealing the artistic license of the *Coronet* story. The details laid out in these autobiographical pieces were supported by quotes from May in the *Christian Science Monitor*, the *New York Herald Tribune*, *Today's Health*, and many other publications during his lifetime.

One of the most important basic facts that the *Coronet* story got wrong concerned when and why *Rudolph* was written. Why was *Rudolph* really written? The answer was pretty straightforward: it was an assignment for Montgomery Ward in 1939. May told Balk in 1963:

> The Red-Nosed Reindeer was born in Chicago when I was working in the advertising copywriting department of Montgomery Ward & Co. . . .
>
> . . . When H. E. MacDonald, the company's retail sales manager, got an idea for a Christmas promotional device for all the company's stores in 1939, he called me in.
>
> "I'd like to provide a little booklet that could be given away to create good will," he said. "I thought of a children's story on the order of Ferdinand the Bull. Could you write a funny little story for us in verse?" I was flabbergasted, but I promptly accepted.[24]

May later noted that he had been given the assignment on a cold, windy day in January.

May also provided a reason why he received the assignment. When the office's Christmas party was approaching in 1937, John A. Martin, a Ward's executive, found himself "woefully short of singers, dancers, and other talent" (though one wonders what kind of office party included dancers).[25] May volunteered. "About the only non-advertising writing I had done were little song parodies to amuse friends at parties. Certainly, few executives of the firm even knew I existed."[26] Martin, after some hesitation, agreed. When May's parodies were well received, he was invited to present more in 1938. Now, at the beginning of 1939, MacDonald, the sales manager, said, "That parody you wrote for the Christmas party wasn't bad. It gave me the idea that maybe you could write some kind of Christmas story that we could use as a giveaway promotion in all our stores next Christmas."[27] MacDonald wanted a story like Munro Leaf's *The Story of Ferdinand*, 1936, about a bull who refuses to fight, written in verse.

In the past, Montgomery Ward had bought coloring books for distribution. May's boss told him, "Look, Bob, Ward stores have been buying crummy little nothings for Christmas giveaways."[28] With each store ordering its own coloring book, there was no overreaching advertising campaign for Ward's. This year, the retail giant (second only to Sears) would create an original in-house product and distribute it through its 620 stores as a unified Christmas promotion. Even though free to the customers, the booklet would save the company the cost of purchasing the coloring books.

May agreed to the assignment, though it was an extra project that would add to his workload. His doubts about the assignment, however, lingered: "Would this be just another gimmick to clutter a holiday landscape already crowded with jolly elves and sugarplum fairies?"[29] He wanted the story to be something more. Still, May's work, life, and finances at the time were complicated by his wife Evelyn's illness. As her condition grew worse, her parents moved into the May household to help out. She nonetheless encouraged May in his new assignment. "She smiled up from her pillow," May later wrote. "'I know it will be great, hon.'"[30]

It was against this backdrop that May began his Christmas story, though it would take many hours—fifty, he estimated—to complete it. He would need to choose the right kind of animal, name him, and then write and rewrite the narrative. Inez Whiteley Foster noted in the *Christian Science Monitor,* "Contrary to popular opinion of the supposedly effortless manner in which commercially salable verse for children is quickly and easily conceived, Mr. May, who is a perfectionist, spent hours and hours of his not-so-free time, chopping and hewing away until his lines sang themselves in dialogue children could naturally recognize as their own."[31] Foster also noted May's early attempts to conceive the story: "For weeks thereafter, Mr. May went around muttering rhymes and discarding well-known fairy folk, until after going through the entire animal kingdom and looking back at unhappy experiences of his own childhood, he finally hit on Rudolph as his inspiration."[32] All these steps—the choice of animal, his name, and the need to convince his boss of the story's worth—would take place over the next eight months.

The choice of what kind of animal May would write about was perhaps his easiest. A reindeer, a staple of Christmas stories, seemed the natural choice, with the added bonus that his daughter Barbara "loved the deer down at the zoo."[33] Other decisions required more thought. May was inspired by the tale of "The Ugly Duckling" and decided to write a story about a deer who is ridiculed for being different; the difference, however, would eventually become an important asset. As May looked out at the fog rolling in from Lake Michigan, he got an idea: How about a deer with eyes that glowed like a cat's, eyes that cut through the night and fog? But perhaps glowing eyes would seem too much like a special power, making the deer a superhero instead of an underdog. Finally, the solution came to May: a shiny red nose that worked like a beacon or train light, clearing a path for Santa's sleigh.

The reindeer, of course, needed a catchy name, and May made a long list of potential names beginning with R: Rodney, Roddy, Roderick, Rudolph, Rudy, Rollo, Roland, Reggy, Reginald, and Romeo. May circled two of these: Rudolph and Reginald. In the end, Reginald simply sounded too British. Rudolph would be the young deer's name.

As May began building the story, he tested it on his daughter Barbara, along with a number of the neighborhood kids. They were his sounding boards, allowing him to make sure the language seemed natural. Although Barbara was only four at the time, she remembered making at least one contribution to *Rudolph*. "My father read me the manuscript of Rudolph, and what I remember was not liking the word stomach. It seemed really icky, so he changed it to tummy."[34]

While May was convinced that he had something special, selling Rudolph to his boss, MacDonald, proved more difficult. MacDonald disliked the original idea, asking May why he was unable to come up with something better. "At first he didn't like the idea of the red nose because it could refer to drinking," MacDonald's wife, Bernice, later said.[35]

May, however, was confident that he had the right idea and only needed to find a way to win over MacDonald. He asked a friend in the art department, Denver Gillen, to make some sketches of deer, and requested that the artist find a way to

Where most reindeers' noses are brownish and tiny,
Poor Rudolph's was red, very large, and quite shiny.

In daylight it dazzled (The picture shows that)
At night time it glowed, like the eyes of a cat.

And putting dirt on it just made it look muddy,
(Oh boy was he mad when they nicknamed him "Ruddy")

Rudolph the Red-Nosed Reindeer, original layout, circa 1939 | Papers of Robert L. May, Rauner Special Collections Library, Dartmouth College; courtesy of Dartmouth College Library

make Rudolph's red nose appealing. May, with Barbara in tow, met Gillen on a Saturday morning at the Lincoln Park Zoo. The first deer that Gillen drew was too old, and May disliked the antlers. The three remained at the park until the afternoon, when Gillen, May believed, had captured the right tone in a number of sketches. "We showed the resulting sketches to MacDonald and the company's art director, and they liked them. The little reindeer had won a reprieve!"[36] The reprieve, however, was only temporary.

It was July, with May on the cusp of finishing Rudolph, when Evelyn died. May's boss offered his sympathy: he would understand if May wanted to put the project

And you", he told Rudolph,"may yet save the day
Your wonderful forehead may yet pave the wa

For a wonderful triumph! It actually might!"
(Old Santa, you notice, was extra polite

To Rudolph, regarding his "wonderful forehead."
To call it a big, shiny nose" would sound horrid!)

Rudolph the Red-Nosed Reindeer, original layout, circa 1939 | Papers of Robert L. May, Rauner Special Collections Library, Dartmouth College; courtesy of Dartmouth College Library

aside. Somebody else at Ward's could finish it. But May was emotionally committed and believed, especially during this time of grief, that he needed Rudolph. He threw himself into the story, laboring over each line until it seemed just right.

For the final test, May called Barbara and Evelyn's parents into the living room and read *Rudolph* to them. "In their eyes," he wrote, "I could see that the story accomplished what I had hoped."[37] Still, *Rudolph* faced opposition at Montgomery Ward. After presenting the story in a meeting to "clerks, secretaries, and others" who worked for MacDonald, May got an earful: "After hearing the story, they expressed strong reservations. Even the idea of a red nose was questioned as having connotations of alcoholism. With each shaft of criticism, my morale sank lower. It looked as if Rudolph might die right there. Then Carl Hacker, the company's display manager spoke up. 'I think that every line that Bob May wrote is beautiful—just perfect,' he said. 'I think it would be a crime for any of us to change one word of it!'"[38]

With Gillen's sketches and a few minor revisions, "The Day before Christmas, or Rudolph the Red-Nosed Reindeer" would become a major promotional campaign for Montgomery Ward in 1939.

Revisiting Rudolph

How, we might ask ourselves some seventy years after the fact, did Frankel and others get the facts so wrong? We might also ask why readers were so willing to believe a story line too good to be true. Perhaps this was just the kind of story that *Coronet*—and later *Good Housekeeping*—readers expected. As Virginia May Herz would later note in an interview, her father was aware of these more romantic versions of Rudolph's origins: "What's out there on the Internet is a softer telling. My dad was aware of it and considered it appropriate. There's the softer, romantic version and the more fact-based version."[39] Even though the softer version of the story has been noted as incorrect by *Snopes*, the Internet site that investigates folklore, myths, and urban legends, the Frankel-Rudolph story continues to circulate as truthful.

Part of the reason for the persistence of the *Coronet* story also rests with journalists and authors accepting these earlier articles as fact-based. In Collins's *Stories behind the Best-Loved Songs of Christmas*, a strong outline of the Frankel article remains. The problem of accepting the previous story is compounded by the fact that many articles about Rudolph were written for the entertainment pages, not as news stories that had to be verified. In the 1940s and 1950s, no one seemed to have bothered speaking to Montgomery Ward employees who had worked with May. No one even bothered to speak to Denver Gillen, whose sketches helped sell *Rudolph* to Ward's. Rudolph, in newspapers and in *Newsweek*, was the stuff of feel-good journalism shaped by the most compelling part of May's story and the limitations of column inches.

It is easy to wonder why May emphasized different details about Rudolph's origin at different points of his life. One recent article by Nate Bloom for *Interfaith Family*, an online magazine that explores Jewish life, focused on May's Jewish background. Bloom suggested that the earliest stories that May told about Rudolph focused on Barbara, his only daughter by his first wife, Evelyn. Bloom underlines that Evelyn, like Robert May, was Jewish. Bloom wrote:

> The fairly important role of his daughter, Barbara, in the creation of the Rudolph poem, is found in articles from 1948 and 1949 about May. Barbara is also given a big role in a 1975 article about the writing of Rudolph. This last article was written by Robert May, himself.
>
> However, Barbara is not mentioned or is given a bare mention in

virtually every other newspaper piece about Rudolph's creation between these dates, including one written by May, himself, in 1963.[40]

In 1941 May married Virginia Newton, a Catholic. Bloom notes that May was later buried in a Catholic cemetery, suggesting that he may have converted. Bloom also suggests that during the years of his marriage to Newton, May choose to de-emphasize his Jewishness. It would only be after Virginia Newton May's death in 1971 that May, once again, returned to the original story:

> It seems pretty clear to me that Robert May wanted to completely bury his Jewish origins. By the 1950s, he wanted to, or was persuaded to, overwrite the existence of his first wife and the role of his daughter Barbara in the creation of Rudolph.
>
> I found it interesting that May just didn't talk about his first wife or Barbara for decades (c. 1950–1973). Then his wife, Virginia, died in 1971. Perhaps with her death, May felt comfortable enough to partially set the record straight for posterity. Without a second spouse looking over his shoulder, in 1975 May authored a new article that gave more detail about the place of his daughter Barbara in Rudolph's creation than any other piece about Rudolph.[41]

While it is easy to admire Bloom's research—his article is one of the most detailed that I have read on May, Johnny Marks, and Rudolph—he perhaps infers more than can be proven. His suggestion that May could have been overly influenced by his second wife to bury details is regrettable. There are many reasons why May might have chosen to emphasize different details at different times.

Another reason for the acceptance of the earlier *Coronet* article, though more speculative, centers on the need for *Rudolph* to spawn its own folklore. *Rudolph* was part of a massive advertising campaign by a major retail chain with a fundamental purpose: to draw consumers into Montgomery Ward who would then purchase other items for Christmas. The softer version of Rudolph, then, strips the red-nosed reindeer of his commercial origins, leaving the impression of a genuine folk article. This lends the Rudolph story an air of authenticity, providing a seamless link between new and old Christmas folklore in America.

As mentioned earlier, it is common for popular stories like *Rudolph* to generate their own folklore—the story about the story. Some details, undoubtedly, are lost over time. *Rudolph the Red-Nosed Reindeer* was a big hit in 1939, but it was only after 1947, when the rights were turned over to May, that more detailed stories began to appear. The *Coronet* article appeared nine years after Montgomery Ward's original promotion, and May's own articles appeared much later. Newspaper and magazine articles would have limited the word count, and in most cases, May probably had little power over what a journalist would emphasize.

Despite all this, it is fairly easy to piece together Rudolph's origins from May's two articles, one written for the *Herald-Journal* in 1963 and the other for *Guideposts* in 1975.

1. May's reputation at Ward's as a writer of song parodies
2. May's assignment of a Christmas promotion project by H. E. MacDonald, Ward's retail sales manager, in January 1939
3. Evelyn May's illness and eventual death in the summer of 1939
4. May's choice of a reindeer for his main character with the name of Rudolph along with a shiny red nose
5. May's decision to base his story on "The Ugly Duckling"; Rudolph would be an underdog
6. May's testing of *Rudolph* on Barbara and her friends
7. MacDonald's initial rejection of the idea
8. Denver Gillen's sketches of deer completed at the Lincoln Zoo to support *Rudolph*
9. The completion of *Rudolph* in late August 1939 and acceptance of *Rudolph* by MacDonald

Even here, I would add a note of caution. While this seems to be as clear an account of Rudolph's origins as we will ever have, the story arc may still leave the impression of being too good to be true. Fighting against the odds for Rudolph,

In spite of the fog, they flew quickly... and low
And made such use of the wonderful glow

From Rudolph's... er... forehead at each intersection
That not even once did they lose their direction!

Rudolph the Red-Nosed Reindeer, original layout, circa 1939 | Papers of Robert L. May, Rauner Special Collections Library, Dartmouth College; courtesy of Dartmouth College Library

May succeeds just as his progeny eventually does in the book. In other words, even "close to the truth" still suggests a mythic quality that de-emphasizes any distracting elements. This story, then, was the story that May chose to tell about Rudolph's origins.

When May turned his project in to MacDonald after finishing in August, it would have been difficult to imagine *Rudolph*'s subsequent longevity. As much as May cared about *Rudolph*, it was a work assignment for Montgomery Ward, and once it was finished, it would be time to move on to other projects. With *Rudolph* ready to be sent to the printers, however, Montgomery Ward planned a Christmas promotion to end all Christmas promotions. Rudolph was just getting started.

two
RUDOLPH'S
FIRST FLIGHT

In the winter of 1939 *Rudolph* made a spectacular debut. Suddenly, a new Christmas story had appeared and seemed, very rapidly, to be accepted as part of a traditional American Christmas. For children who had gathered up the nearly two and a half million copies of *Rudolph* from Ward's, these books would be dusted off, read, and reread the following Christmas; for younger children, it was the perfect accompaniment while sitting on Mom's or Dad's lap. *Rudolph* also paired easily with Clement C. Moore's "A Visit from St. Nicholas," giving parents a new classic to read aloud in the family living room on chilly December evenings.

The original *Rudolph* more closely resembled a pamphlet or comic book than a hardbound children's book, and these softcover versions can be quite valuable today. A parent could easily roll the thirty-two-page booklet into Junior's or Sis's stocking. When the book was opened on Christmas morning, the color layout must have made a striking first impression: for retail catalogs and even *Life* magazine, color was still fairly novel. Yet here was a colorfully laid out book, not a book to be colored. Perhaps this seemed like common sense for Ward's: How could you have a book about a red-nosed reindeer if the illustrations were in black and white? Clearly, the clean layout and Denver Gillen's cheerful drawings caught the eye.

Rudolph grabbed attention in other ways: even before a child learns of Rudolph's misfortunes, she sees something very peculiar. In the first drawing, young reindeer are playing in a winter wonderland, skating with skates on their hooves, sliding on the ice with protective pillows, and riding sleds down the hillside. One reindeer even climbs a tree. The scene looks a little like a prototype for the opening of *A Charlie Brown Christmas* (1965), with the young reindeer playing just as children play on the ice. Two adult reindeer stand on the sidelines watching, one with a pair of glasses, another with a pipe and scarf. These reindeer, young and old, act pretty much like any other adults and children in the wintertime.

As Tim Hollis wrote in *Christmas Wishes*, this may be one of the first examples of Santa's reindeer being given human characteristics. "With no apparent prior model," wrote Hollis, "May decided to have his reindeer characters live in houses and speak English, both among themselves and to humans such as Santa Claus."[1] Like Beatrix Potter's *Peter Rabbit* or Hans Christian Andersen's "The Ugly Duckling," *Rudolph* joined a growing body of children's literature with anthropomorphic animals. Reindeer, once relegated to pulling Santa's sleigh in silence, could now develop rounded personalities.

Another surprise, for those familiar only with the Gene Autry song or Rankin/Bass's *Rudolph* (1964), is that May's original story was in fact a poem. "Twas the day before Christmas, and all through the hills / The reindeer were playing . . . enjoying the spills."[2] Though May's source of inspiration was Clement Moore's "A Visit from St. Nicholas" (1823), the use of verse was perhaps unusual for children's literature at the time. May's opening line mimics Moore's famous poem ("'Twas the night before Christmas, when all through the house / Not a creature was stirring, not even a mouse"[3]) and follows with the same meter. The rhyme and length of each line imbue the poem with the sing-songy flow of a classic nursery rhyme.

May's literary choices define the target audience: young children. Parents may make an appearance in *Rudolph*, but they play small roles. This is primarily a children's book about childhood experience, and parents—save for the childlike Santa Claus—stay on the sidelines.

May's original story also included a number of idiosyncrasies that may have been lost in the shuffle of later versions of *Rudolph*, including cartoons, comic books, animated specials, and two movies. Not only do Rudolph and the other reindeer speak English, but Rudolph is quite capable of writing a note; later, his parents are shown reading it. May's reindeer reside in houses, have separate bedrooms, and sleep in beds (in the Rankin/Bass special in 1964, for instance, reindeer seem to live in caves). Instead of living at the North Pole, Rudolph lives in a rural village with other reindeer families. Rudolph has parents, which we see only later in the story, but they are never named. In May's story, then, Rudolph is not the son of Donner (as in the Rankin/Bass special) or the son of Blitzen (in another version). As in most stories about Rudolph, Gillen gets a basic reindeer fact wrong: he leaves the impression that males have antlers, while females are antlerless. Reindeer, however, are an exception to this rule: during winter, female reindeer keep their antlers, while males lose them.[4]

Even at the North Pole, where Santa's first reindeer team resides, the reindeer behave more like people than deer. The reindeer team sits on long benches at a table, eating a meal before the Christmas flight. The reindeer have plates, silverware, and glasses. They also have good manners: each has a napkin around his neck. One oddity is that May seems to assume that reindeer, if they wish, can fly. No one in Rudolph's village is seen flying early in the book, but Santa Claus's reindeer at the North Pole clearly can fly. When Santa Claus asks Rudolph to help out, there is never a question of whether he can fly: this is simply accepted.

There is one important though less noticeable change in May's story when compared to earlier Christmas narratives: as James H. Barnett has noted in *The American Christmas*, Santa Claus has limited powers in *Rudolph*. Traditionally, Santa Claus has been more like a god: he knows whether children have been naughty or nice, and he knows whether they are sleeping or awake. In *Rudolph*, however, Santa faces problems that he is incapable of solving by himself. Early in his Christmas flight, we see Santa's sleigh tangled in a tree, with Santa himself jostled from his seat. On the same page, Santa faces a more modern problem: he and his sleigh team are nearly hit by a trimotor plane. At one house, Santa, looking for a chimney, slips and skins his knee; inside the house, he knocks the dishes from the sink. In *Rudolph*, Santa Claus faces multiple dangers, along with the threat of bodily harm. Santa can deliver all the toys to all the children of the world in one night, but his eyesight cannot penetrate fog or see in the dark any better than anyone else's. Because of this, May's Santa Claus seems more human than Moore's. Santa may have special talents, but he clearly needs Rudolph to fulfill his Christmas Eve mission.

The bare bones of May's story line in *Rudolph* have remained ever since. Rudolph is kind and modest, your average reindeer next door. Average, that is, except for his unusual nose, which leads other reindeer to make fun of him. Like the ugly duckling, however, Rudolph is more than he seems, for it is his nose that allows him (the child) to save Santa (the adult) on a foggy night. Rudolph's heroic flight and Santa's praise also trigger a change of heart in the other reindeer: now they envy the red-nosed reindeer. *Rudolph the Red-Nosed Reindeer* is the story of an American hero.

May's Rudolph seemed tailor-made for these late Depression years, a children's fairy tale that captured the exuberance of the American spirit. Rudolph promised to inspire American children during a dark hour (they too could help, just like Rudolph) while winning the approval of Mom and Dad. These qualities—modesty and a can-do attitude—also made Rudolph the perfect spokesman for Montgomery Ward during the holiday season of 1939. As Rudolph's bright beacon quickly cut through the fog that threatened Christmas Eve, it also promised to light the way and increase the bottom line of one retail giant.

Promoting Rudolph

In the fall of 1939, Montgomery Ward prepared for a Christmas promotion to end all Christmas promotions: Rudolph the Red-Nosed Reindeer, a brand-new holiday character, would be unveiled to the American public. As an in-house promotion poster read, "Get ready for Rudolph the Red-Nosed Reindeer. The rollickingest, rip-roaringest, riot-provokingest, Christmas give-away your town has ever seen!"[5] At the center of the Ward promotion would be Robert L. May's original work, *Rudolph the Red-Nosed Reindeer*, with Denver Gillen's drawings: "A big, thick, 32-page book . . . printed in 4 gay colors throughout! An amusing, exciting new

Christmas story, written in rollicking verse! A laugh and a thrill for every boy and girl in your town (and for their *parents*, too!) They'll come a-runnin' . . . for the best Christmas-traffic-producer we've ever seen or heard of! You'll receive your supply about December 1st."[6] While the author of this promotional poster remains anonymous, it is intriguing to wonder whether May himself—as a copywriter—helped prepare material for the Rudolph campaign at Ward's. The sheer number of booklets—2.4 million—dwarfed the printing of any children's book by a publisher at the time.

By 1939 Montgomery Ward stood as a powerhouse of American retail, second only to Sears, blanketing the forty-eight states and territories with 620 stores. The Depression years, however, offered substantial challenges. Following an $8.7 million loss in 1931, Ward's had recruited

"Get Ready for Rudolph the Red-Nosed Reindeer," Montgomery Ward in-house promotion poster, circa 1939 | Papers of Robert L. May, Rauner Special Collections Library, Dartmouth College; courtesy of Dartmouth College Library

"Gloomy" Sewell Avery, known for his knack at turning a profit during economic downturns. After closely scrutinizing the competition (Sears) and bringing in new department heads, Avery and his new staff quickly rebuilt retail and catalog sales. In 1937 Ward's cleared over $23 million from $414 million in sales. These impressive profits also revealed the changing landscape of retail. Early in its history, Ward's had focused on catalog sales. Increasingly, however, the retail stores—initiated in 1926 at Ward's—were generating greater profits. The in-store promotion of Rudolph promised to take advantage of this fact.

Despite an upturn in Ward's fortunes, the broader world into which Rudolph would be introduced was an anxious one in 1939. While many believed the Depression would soon be over, unemployment remained high; as Gary Cross has written, "The unemployment rate never dropped below 7.7 million (14.3 percent) during the 1930s."[7] The language used by *Coronet* to describe May and his family's "lowly" circumstances in 1938 could have easily described the typical American experience during these years. The shrunken economy battered the poor while also deflating the middle class: an education at Dartmouth, like Robert May's, no longer guaranteed success. "What was new after 1929," wrote Steven Mintz and Susan Kellogg in *Domestic Revolutions*, "was that the trauma of joblessness and loss of property began to affect families that had previously felt immune from such fears."[8] Because of underemployment and unemployment, many Americans waited to get married, while married couples delayed having children. Families like May's still aspired to home ownership and filling that home with children and the latest appliances, but the dream would have to be put on hold until better times.

Despite hard times, Christmas remained central to the American way of life and the most important time of the year for retailers like Montgomery Ward. Even as families scraped together resources for necessities, wish books by companies like Ward's offered easy access to an enormous variety of goods. Any innovative promotion offered the chance of pulling customers from Sears, Macy's, and other retail stores. Even with big plans, however, Ward's and other retailers faced one other obstacle: in 1939, there was a great deal of confusion over Thanksgiving. Traditionally, Thanksgiving had been celebrated on the last Thursday in November. Because Thanksgiving would have fallen on the very last day of November in 1939, President Roosevelt, to give the economy a boost, decided to change the date of the celebration to the fourth Thursday of November. Roosevelt's change, however, had no binding force on individual states. As a result, some Americans celebrated on the traditional day, while others celebrated "Franksgiving." For the retail world, this was confusing. With "the perfect Christmas crowd-bringer!" Montgomery Ward was counting on Rudolph to save the day.[9]

"December 1939 . . . Promotional Service," Montgomery Ward, circa 1939 | Papers of Robert L. May, Rauner Special Collections Library, Dartmouth College; courtesy of Dartmouth College Library

The Psychology of Toys

Beginning in September, the retail sales department began contacting store managers within the Montgomery Ward network about holiday promotions. This explains why May *had* to finish the *Rudolph* manuscript by August: this would allow time for printing and shipping the book to individual stores. Within Ward's, there was a push to get everyone on board: retail sales wanted everyone excited about Rudolph. Even with Sewell Avery's dedicated executives, each of Ward's 620 stores was operated by individual managers. A September memo made the pitch to these managers, providing the same logic for the promotion as H. E. MacDonald had given May at the beginning of the year:

> Many stores in the past have used, as Christmas give-aways, a
> miscellaneous assortment of balloons, whistles, buttons, and what-not . . .
> with each store working entirely on its own. These give-aways have been
> cheap . . . and have *looked* cheap!
>
> We have given considerable thought to this subject, have carefully
> analyzed the give-aways that we and our competitors have used in the
> past, and have reached the conclusion that this problem can be dealt
> with far better, from every angle, if Wards stores plan and *order together,
> through this department.*[10]

The promotion of *Rudolph*, then, would require a new outlook for Montgomery Ward, a unified front that would reverberate through every store and throughout the retail world.

Montgomery Ward worked hard to get all 620 stores focused on Rudolph, encouraging stores to "run 'em regularly [newspaper ads], and reap the profit . . . in traffic!"[11] Each store would also receive two fifty-seven-by-eighteen-inch Rudolph displays, "in an eye-catching 4-color combination of red, green, brown and black."[12] For the December issue of *Business Builder*, an in-house magazine, Rudolph was featured on the cover, perhaps one of the first images of the red-nosed reindeer leading Santa's team. Santa and the reindeer team are flying over a Mont-

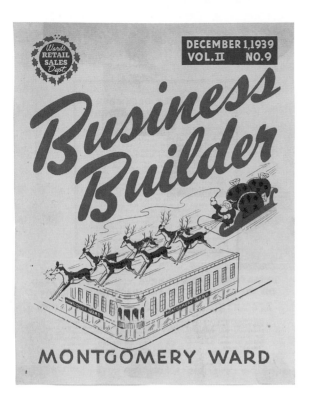

Montgomery Ward's
Business Builder, December
1, 1939 | Papers of Robert
L. May, Rauner Special
Collections Library,
Dartmouth College;
courtesy of Dartmouth
College Library

27
*Rudolph's
First Flight*

gomery Ward store, and four of the reindeer are labeled: Rudolph, Newspaper Ads, Circulars, and Displays. Interestingly, Santa is carrying huge bags of money, the results—no doubt—of a properly executed marketing campaign. Inside, the magazine offered:

> As for "Rudolph" . . . he is the hero whose adventures on Christmas Eve are related in "Rudolph, the Red Nosed Reindeer." A thousand copies of this book have been mailed to each office. They are our Christmas gift to the children and you'll want to give a copy to your customers who have children and to any child who comes in the Office accompanied by an adult. To avoid wasting the books, do not give a copy to a child, unless

"A Message from
Rudolph," cover, circa
1939 | Montgomery
Ward Collection,
Box 44, Folder 3,
American Heritage
Center, University
of Wyoming

there is an adult along. Of course, you can make exceptions to the rule in particular cases.[13]

Santa Claus remained a prominent fixture at Montgomery Ward in 1939, but Rudolph would be on equal footing.

Part of the push required precision timing. Individual stores had to place their order early so that the paper for every book that would be printed could be purchased at the same time. This one-batch purchase would save money. Also, each store would incur the cost of the purchased booklets: no more than one and a half cents per copy of *Rudolph*: "We believe even the smallest BC store should order at least 1,000 . . . a mere $15 worth. With the intensive promotion the book will receive in our newspaper and circular advertising, we believe that

the medium-to-large 'B' store will require from 3,000 to 5,000 ($45 to $75 worth). 'A' stores should run anywhere from 10,000 up."[14] These letters referred to different-size Montgomery Ward stores. Bigger ('A') stores were complete department stores, while the others had more limited lines. For all these stores, Ward's sales department worked hard to promote the cost benefits to store managers: "We believe that an exclusive story like this, aggressively advertised in our newspaper ads and circulars . . . can bring every store an incalculable amount of publicity . . . and, far more important, a tremendous amount of Christmas traffic. Traffic, not only for Toys, but for *every* department in your store. Not only children, of course, but their parents as well."[15]

It is interesting to compare the cost of these booklets with the cost of catalogs, still a major part of Ward's strategy for rural customers. In 1939 Ward's printed seven million fall catalogs at the cost of one dollar each. Compared to overhead for catalog printing, *Rudolph* was a very inexpensive proposition.

For other in-house literature, Ward's offered more specific ideas about promoting *Rudolph*:

1. Give the book away ONLY to children accompanied by adults. This will limit "street urchin" traffic to a minimum, and will bring-in the PARENTS . . . the people you want to sell!
2. Make sure that your main-floor sales-clerks are familiar with the place (or places) where the book is being given away . . . so that they may direct customers accordingly.
3. If dates permit, make conspicuous use of Rudolph (in ads and displays) in connection with your Toy Department Opening, and with any Christmas Parade your town may hold.
4. You have already received one advance copy of this book, along with a return-form for ordering an additional supply. It is our opinion that the quantities originally ordered by many stores will prove insufficient to permit promoting the book aggressively during the whole Christmas season. If you believe this to be the case in your store . . . please order your additional supply at once.[16]

The promotion and marketing personnel at Ward had mapped out its campaign in great detail.

Besides store managers, Ward's focused on the ground troops who would make the sale. An in-house pamphlet titled "A Message from Rudolph" sold the holiday season to sales clerks as "your big opportunity for increased earnings through Wards Personal Production Compensation Plan."[17] Inside the first page an inscription read, "Each employee is expected to read carefully and to put into practice all of the suggestions in this message."[18] Employees were entreated to work hard and be selfless like Rudolph, and to "Sell in the Spirit of Christmas": "Picture the happiness that your customers will bring to their friends and families as they select toys, radios, electric refrigerators, furnishings, and clothing. *See*

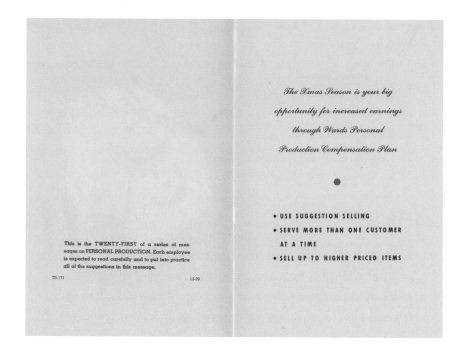

The Xmas Season is your big opportunity for increased earnings through Wards Personal Production Compensation Plan

- USE SUGGESTION SELLING
- SERVE MORE THAN ONE CUSTOMER AT A TIME
- SELL UP TO HIGHER PRICED ITEMS

This is the TWENTY-FIRST of a series of messages on PERSONAL PRODUCTION. Each employee is expected to read carefully and to put into practice all of the suggestions in this message.

TR-171   12-39

"A Message from Rudolph," opening pages, circa 1939 | Montgomery Ward Collection, Box 44, Folder 3, American Heritage Center, University of Wyoming

the merchandise in use; and the pleasure it will bring. Such attitudes will build an interest in others, and make your Christmas selling an adventure—exciting and thrilling."[19] Through hard work and the right attitude, the troops—with a little help from Rudolph—would deliver the bottom line for Ward's.

One aspect of the campaign that might seem shortsighted today is that the promotion of Rudolph failed to include any direct merchandizing. In time, however, Rudolph's image would grace a variety of toys and products for kids. Disney pioneered tie-ins and cross-promotions in the 1930s with Mickey Mouse, Pinocchio, and Snow White.[20] Ward's, however, moved more cautiously. The *Rudolph* book would bring children and parents into Montgomery Ward to purchase toys that the company already stocked.

The line between *Rudolph* as a book and *Rudolph* as an advertisement nonetheless remained razor thin. *Rudolph* would delight children, *and* the book would sell

A Message from Rudolph

HAVE you read the tale of "Rudolph—The Red-Nosed Reindeer"? It's ten to one you have! And if you have, it's twenty to one you'll read it again — and again. And if you have children, it's almost an absolute certainty that you'll keep on reading it!

For what person—adult or child—can resist such lines as:

While every so often they'd stop to call names
At one little deer not allowed in their games:

"Ha ha! Look at Rudolph! His nose is a sight!"
"It's red as a beet!" "Twice as *big!*" "Twice as *bright!*"

Where *most* reindeer' noses are brownish and tiny,
Poor Rudolph's was red, very large, and quite shiny.

In daylight it dazzled. (The *picture* shows that!)
At night-time it glowed, like the eyes of a cat.

3

Rudolph Delivers the Goods

Well, as you know, Rudolph's greatest handicap — his shiny red nose — became his greatest asset, as he led the way through the fog that was delaying Santa on Christmas Eve to the "houses and streets" until "the very last stocking was filled to the top, *just* as the sun was preparing to pop."

★

The job was so well done that Santa said:

"Rudolph, I *never* have had
A deer quite so brave or so brilliant as you
At fighting black fog, and at guiding me through.

By *YOU* last night's journey was *actually* bossed.
Without you, I'm certain we'd all have been lost!

I hope you'll continue to keep us from grief,
On *future* dark trips, as COMMANDER-IN-CHIEF!"

4

Your Christmas Opportunity

Christmas furnishes the opportunity of a lifetime for *you* to save countless shoppers from grief. Literally, you can become the "Commander-in-Chief" as you *suggest* the right gift, and make certain that the customer doesn't leave the Store until her Christmas needs are filled.

Rudolph gained renown and the gratitude of all because he put zest, dash, and enthusiasm into what he did with what he had. Just as you can!

A dreary, spiritless performance is bad enough at any time. But at Christmas, when we're all in an unselfish atmosphere of giving, there is an extra incentive for all of us to do our very best.

Rudolph-like, let's get the spirit of doing a Christmas-like job. To do this, get a picture of the person to whom the gift is to be given. You'll discover so much that's interesting and worth-while.

5

Many a young lady will come to the Men's Furnishings Department with face all aglow. If you have imagination and the right interest in your opportunity, you may discover that she wants a shirt for her boy friend — that the young folks are engaged, and that she thinks he takes a size 15½, for he's six feet four inches tall, weighs 200 pounds and has freckles and red hair. Help her pick a tie, too, and a handkerchief that will fold nicely for his coat pocket.

*T * T*

Sell in the Spirit of Christmas

Picture the happiness that your customers will bring to their friends and families as they select toys, radios, electric refrigerators, furnishings, and clothing. *See the merchandise in use; and the pleasure it will bring.* Such attitudes will build an interest in others, and make your Christmas selling an adventure — exciting and thrilling.

6

With what "umph" you can display these gifts. What a dramatic touch you can give the sale by the deft, almost affectionate manner in which you handle and display the merchandise that is to become "Somebody's Christmas Present." Through such showmanship and service — plus, the desirability of the merchandise can be conveyed to customers to such a degree that they'll feel, "Let me have it quick. That's the gift I need."

Service, the right attitude, and a desire to do his best, brought Rudolph the envy of all, far and near—

> For *no* greater honor can come to a deer.
> Than riding with Santa and guiding his sleigh!
> The number-one job, on the number-one day!

We, too, in serving Wards millions of customers have the Number One Job in the Number One Season! How exciting this job is, and what satisfaction it can bring as we think of giving our best to help others in the greatest giving season of the year. Our willingness to

7

be patient, kind, considerate, and to see that our customers fill *all* their needs in the *best* and *most satisfactory* way, will *light the way* to the hearts of millions of anxious men, women, and children.

Truly the message conveyed in the story of Rudolph (if the fun of reading the story doesn't cover up the fact that there may be a message there) can be taken completely to heart by "U"—Wards Salesforce.

8

toys. *Business Builder* offered the following advice for employees: "From now until Christmas, Toys will be one of your top rank 'Volume Getters.' Here's why: in about 90% of American homes, toys are on the 'must' gift list . . . and you have, in the Christmas catalog, one of the largest and most complete assortments the country affords. It is, in fact, the largest that Wards have ever presented."[21] The story of the young reindeer with the shiny nose would simply guide Mom and Dad with Junior and Sis in tow to the Montgomery Ward toy department. Once the family was drawn into the store, Ward's clerks could make the holiday sale.

Ward's *Business Builder* also reminded employees that the toy business was no longer for amateurs. It offered specific advice on selling toys to children in an article titled "The Psychology of Toys": "Don't let anyone tell you that toys are a 'Natural' and will sell themselves. Today, child psychology has entered this market and cha[n]ged, not only the merchandise, but the technique of selling it."[22] Now toys were capable of more than entertaining children—they also added to a child's development. Parents, through magazines

"A Message from Rudolph," back cover, circa 1939 | Montgomery Ward Collection, Box 44, Folder 3, American Heritage Center, University of Wyoming

and radio, understood this. "The clever salesperson, therefore, will learn what the authorities on child psychology say about selecting the right toys and adapt his selling to it."[23] A good sales clerk knew how to select a toy that was right for a child's age, that "encourages him to do and learn something," that is "durable and safe," that does "what [it's] supposed to do," and promote the more durable toys over the cheaper ones by noting that they will last longer.[24]

Even with the entire Montgomery Ward family on board, the company needed to spread the word to the broader public. A massive campaign would be waged to enlist newspapers in order to raise public awareness of Rudolph. Without it, thousands of copies of *Rudolph the Red-Nosed Reindeer* would remain in cardboard boxes at individual stores.

Montgomery Ward reached out to newspapers throughout the forty-eight states (and probably beyond), seemingly requesting free space for a story about the *Rudolph* giveaway. A letter from John A. Martin, a space buyer for Ward's, outlined many of the same points that would appear in article after article on *Rudolph* in the winter of 1939. After noting the basic facts—that Montgomery Ward planned to give away a Christmas booklet, and that 2.4 million copies were available—the letter included the kind of details that make good copy. Under the letter's third point, Martin noted,

> The book has barely started circulating . . . yet is already causing a
> sensation: - -
> A. Teachers and psychologists are hailing it as the perfect Christmas
>   book for children . . . with the result that we are receiving school
>   requests by the thousand.
> B. John Barrymore requested an autographed copy, and changed the
>   script of his current play, "My Dear Children," to include a mention of
>   "Rudolph."
> C. The publishers of the book made a vain attempt to buy the rights for
>   next year . . . . expressing the opinion that it's a cinch for the movies.
>   (We're inclined to agree with them.)
> D. And getting down to *real authorities*, my own 5-year-old offspring
>   expressed the opinion that "'Rudolph's got 'Ferdinand the Bull'
>   and 'The Night Before Christmas' beat a mile!" (And who am *I*
>   to disagree?)[25]

It did not matter who these teachers, experts, and psychologists were: newspapers repeated Martin's "facts." Word spread quickly through local newspapers, notifying children and parents to hurry to get a copy of *Rudolph the Red-Nosed Reindeer*.

By the Christmas season of 1939, Montgomery Ward had laid the groundwork for a novel and substantial promotion. Managers and management obviously believed they had a story that kids would love and parents would embrace. Newspaper articles had been run, displays had been placed in stores, and circulars had circulated. *Rudolph the Red-Nosed Reindeer* was printed in Poughkeepsie, New York, and the retail sales department wrote, "We are very much pleased with the result; we sincerely hope that *you* are, too."[26] Montgomery Ward had done everything in its power to guarantee that Rudolph's first flight would be a success.

Rudolph's Reception

"'Rudolph the Red-Nosed Reindeer' is a child's book that is making history," wrote the *Arizona Daily Star*.[27] This publicity, no doubt, helped move a large number of books in a very short time (between December 1 and Christmas); for stores that had ordered too few copies, supplies were quickly depleted. Requests poured in, from individuals, schools, and other organizations, for more copies. In all probability, Ward's printed too few copies of *Rudolph*.

The number of booklets given away was impressive: 2,365,016. A map, perhaps made by Ward's or May, broke down Rudolph giveaways by individual states and regions.

The "Distribution of Rudolph" map revealed that 117,200 copies had been distributed in Pennsylvania, 101,000 in New York, and 27,000 in Virginia. At 236,016 copies, Illinois gave away the most (Ward's headquarters was located in Chicago); at 1,000 copies, Washington, D.C., and Delaware gave away the fewest.

There were regional differences, but there are no data to measure this against Montgomery Ward's presence in a given state or region. (The map fails to define Ward's five regions, so I have referred to traditional regional divisions.) In the Deep South, for instance, South Carolina, Georgia, and Alabama each gave away only 5,000 copies. It is possible, however, that catalog sales were more important than retail sales for Ward's in the rural South, leading to lower numbers. The

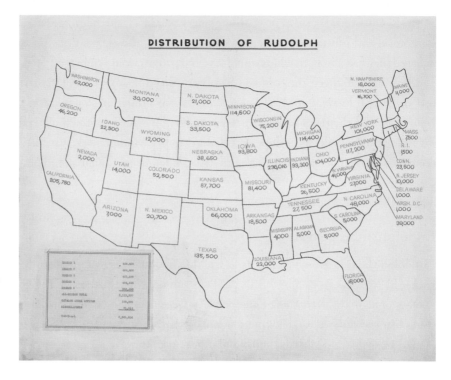

DISTRIBUTION OF RUDOLPH

only detail that makes these aberrations odd is that surrounding states with rural populations gave away many more copies. Against South Carolina's 5,000, for instance, North Carolina gave away 48,000 copies. In the West, similar splits occurred. In Nevada, for instance, only 2,000 copies were distributed; in Utah, 14,000. However one crunched these numbers, though, Rudolph had saturated the forty-eight states.

The vast number of copies, however, only proved that Montgomery Ward had successfully promoted and given away nearly two and a half million copies of *Rudolph the Red-Nosed Reindeer*. And while a number of newspaper articles praised *Rudolph*, most only repeated Ward's publicity. It was letters, from newspaper editors, schoolteachers, and the students themselves, that measured just how deeply Americans had taken Rudolph to heart.

Fan Letters

Following *Rudolph*'s introduction, congratulatory letters poured in to Ward's. While friends wrote to congratulate May, many of the letters concerning Rudolph were addressed to John Martin or Ward's in general; even though May's name appeared on the booklet, many attributed the book to the Montgomery Ward advertising department. Indeed, even in the newspaper campaign, neither May's nor Gillen's name assumed central importance. May was simply another copywriter and part of a larger team; with the exception of recognition from friends, it would take time for May's name to come to the forefront.

A number of letters requested copies of the book. "Please autograph a copy of Rudolph to Cornelius Vanderbilt Jr.," wrote Jack Story.[28] George Smith, a friend, wrote to congratulate May: "Just saw your opus on 'Rudy the Red.' . . . It's a grand job—perfectly swell. Wire Disney! . . . Call Max Fleischer! It's tops. It's as fine as anything I've ever seen in the kiddie field. I for one predict a wide acclaim for the four-legged W. C. Fields."[29] M. Herbert Baker offered further praise. "Your splendid contribution to American literature is receiving the appreciation it richly deserves."[30] And from Dartmouth, Sidney Hayward offered, "Everything has stopped for me this morning while I have read and reread your inspired and perfectly grand 'Rudolph.'"[31]

Other letters were simply entertaining, including an exchange that took place between Raymond Dobson, a newspaper advertising manager, and May. Dobson addressed his letter to Martin, the ad-space buyer for Montgomery Ward:

Rudolph, the Red-Nosed Reindeer, got in through the front door of the Dobson home and caused a lot of complications. He was found at your local store.

If you have an explanation that I can give my four-year-old boy and three-year-old girl as to why the deer in the Minot [North Dakota] zoo do not have red noses like Rudolph, please send them along by airmail special delivery.

I haven't been able to explain it to their satisfaction, and I am getting a bit weary of being asked to make repeat trips to the zoo to see whether Rudolph has taken up abode there.[32]

May easily stepped into the role of Rudolph's father:

As Rudolph's father, and Montgomery Wards' authority on deer, I was given your letter to John Martin, and asked to solve the very knotty problem presented by the absence of red-nosed reindeer in the Minot zoo.

I recommend that you try to sell your children on the idea that Rudolph is the only red-nosed reindeer in existence. (That's why Santa Claus found him of such unique assistance.) Rudolph's year round habitat, of course, is in the hilly home town set forth in the book. Santa Claus would never permit him to be installed in a zoo. After all, a zoo isn't much fun! Rudolph spends the greater part of the year playing around the hills and woods with his companions (who no longer call him names). At Christmas, of course . . . or, at least, whenever it's foggy . . . Rudolph is summoned to join Santa and the rest of the reindeer at the North Pole, so that Rudolph's shiny schnozzle can light the way through the darkness and mist.[33]

Quickly, it seems, *Rudolph* was becoming a real part of Christmas lore, expanding beyond the confines of the booklet.

While *Rudolph* was clearly aimed at children, the story line was one that could be easily embraced by parents. And while *Rudolph* teaches a lesson that most parents would have found appropriate, the appeal of the book ran deeper. One letter sent from the *Sandusky Times* explained the appeal of *Rudolph* to adults: "When the copy . . . came to my desk it took me back to the days when I sat on my father's lap by the fireside and he would recite to me 'It was the Night Before Christmas' and when my grandchildren came I did the same thing."[34] Another letter, from Melvin Taylor to John Martin, read: "Thank you for 'Rudolph The Red-Nosed Reindeer.' Of course the first thing I did was to very casually present it before the junior members of the testing laboratory I maintain (three of them) and the result has unseated 'Peter Rabbit' from the lofty perch it has occupied in the Taylor household."[35] One other newspaper editor wrote, "I have a five-year-old boy at home who's well acquainted with the fog-piercing ability of the reindeer's red nose."[36] Rudolph, overflowing his place as a character in a book for children, was warmly embraced by the entire family.

Educators also wrote, both approving of *Rudolph* as Christmas literature and requesting more copies. In Glencoe, Illinois, reading counselor Ruby M. Schuyler wrote of *Rudolph*, "We are delighted with this book as a contribution to the Christmas literature for children and we are eager to make it available to the children who attend our schools."[37] Once again, Montgomery Ward probably underestimated the demand, or perhaps never imagined distributing the book to schools (it was the parents, after all, that Ward's wished to bring into the store). At least one Ward's store, however, in Bakersfield, California, did just that: 6,440 copies of *Rudolph* were distributed to fifteen schools. One teacher wrote, "As I am a First-Grade teacher, and could make such good use of it [*Rudolph*], I would like to secure a copy."[38]

Both the volume and tone of these responses must have been heartening to May and Montgomery Ward, but perhaps the most appreciated responses came from the children themselves. One came from a fourth grader named Susan and was addressed to Miss Schuyler, the reading counselor: "Thank you for coming to fourth grade, and reading the poem of 'Rudolf the Reindeer.' I thought it was a very nice poem. Have you ever heard of any other Reindeer beside Rudolf with a red nose? I have not."[39] Another letter, from a boy named Howard, stated, "We all think that 'Rudolf, The Reindeer' is one of the best Christmas stories we had ever heard and I wish I had one."[40] Even though Rudolph had just celebrated his first flight with Santa Claus, he had quickly become an essential part of the Christmas celebration for many Americans.

Business Possibilities

As bold as Ward's move may have been, one could argue that it should have been bolder: no merchandizing accompanied the original Rudolph promotion. In retrospect, at least, this appears shortsighted. By the end of the 1930s, it had become more common for businesses to promote fictional characters. Walt Disney, in particular, supported feature-length cartoons with promotional campaigns and merchandise tie-ins. While Disney made sure that Mickey Mouse's image never appeared on an ashtray, the mouse that even Mom and Dad loved appeared on everything else. By 1939—the year *Rudolph* came out—Disney had perfected the mass campaign and product tie-ins: although *Pinocchio* would not reach theaters until February 1940, marketable merchandise was in production during the summer of 1939. While Ward's initially utilized Rudolph for little more than to lure children with parents into its stores, the retail giant would quickly see a world of possibilities for its new Christmas character. Still, this delayed response probably shortened both Rudolph's reach and the company's profits.[41]

It was only after gauging the public's response that Ward's began to consider a broader role for Rudolph. For a number of managers at Ward's, the next step seemed obvious: extend the promotion to the following year (or years). J. Knowles, an assistant manager at a Ward's store in Traverse City, Michigan, wrote: "The display man of our store made the suggestion that this story could easily be promoted into a new fairy tale for our company through the distribution of the same story for several years. The acceptance of this story among our customers, young and old, is tremendous. This would give us an exclusive story on which we could very easily capitolise [*sic*] by manufacturing a stuffed toy, or one of such type, of Rudolph the Red Nosed Reindeer. We have had several requests from customers for said toy."[42]

Meanwhile, other ideas on how to develop Rudolph came from movie studios and book publishers. Like Ferdinand the Bull or Mickey Mouse, Rudolph seemed a natural for cartoons, merchandize tie-ins, and book publishers. As 1939 spilled into 1940, other suggestions were offered. "We [Ward's] put 'Rudolph' into the hands of approximately 3,000,000 people last year. Here is a 'natural.' What better build up could any movie actor want? Walt Disney would jump at an actor with the publicity 'Rudolph' already has. Each Christmas season Disney could make a short movie of the adventures of Rudolph of the previous year, thereby not interfering with our current story."[43] While this may have seemed like an over-the-top suggestion compared to a stuffed toy, the involvement of Disney was not out of the question in 1940. In fact, Montgomery Ward received letters from more than one movie studio, suggesting just that. In some cases, however, the idea had received help. John Rose, writing from Disney studios at the beginning of 1940, was responding to a letter from May. Another letter, from Irving Heineman Jr. with Looney Tunes, was likewise a response. While the letters expressed interest, potential problems emerged that seemed likely to derail any Rudolph side-project. Heineman's letter, in particular, contains a humorous opening in the guise of an apology: "I am writing this myself because if it is dictated the whole damned studio will know about it before the letter is mailed. Its [*sic*] just one of those things. Nothing happens in a studio without everyone including the janitor knowing more about it than the parties concerned."[44] The complications of a Rudolph cartoon, however, were outlined. There would be no payment for the book, save that "fifty million people a week see our cartoons."[45] Further, Montgomery Ward would not be given screen credit, Heineman explained, because the Hayes Office (the organization that oversaw movie content) would turn it down because "it smacked of advertising."[46] At the beginning of 1940, Rudolph's road to movie-star status seemed full of potholes.

Other opportunities, more squarely aimed toward May, seemed more realistic. At the beginning of 1940, May received a letter from the publishers Alfred Knopf and Random House, both complimenting and encouraging him, though making no commitment. One editor noted to a colleague, "I think Mr. May's RUDOLPH is amusing, and I should think he could do a good juvenile. Why doesn't he try one. Not in rhyme, though—not much of a market for that!"[47] Another letter mentions the possibility of having *Rudolph* turned into a sound recording at Victor. In many of these cases, once again, it appears that May perhaps made first contact.

While there were many wild cards in the mix, one thing seemed certain: Rudolph, at the beginning of 1940, was the hit of the holiday season. And this was a fact that Montgomery Ward, in the midst of the Depression, must have been keenly aware of. While Rudolph might eventually make his way to recordings, commercial books, and even the movies, the idea with the most traction was for Ward's to expand its Rudolph campaign into the Christmas season of 1940. At the beginning of 1940, this is exactly what it planned to do.

three
PREPARING FOR RUDOLPH'S SECOND FLIGHT

Realizing that they had tapped into something much bigger than they had imagined, Montgomery Ward initially planned an even bigger coming-out party for Rudolph in 1940. In a March letter-memo to store managers, the retail sales department wrote:

Everyone we have checked-with shares our belief that "Rudolph" in 1940 will play a far bigger, more important role than in 1939. Here are the reasons why:

1. As we have already stated, a great many stores ordered insufficient quantities last year, and were unable to fill all requests . . . particularly from schools. (Incidentally, stores who *did* order enough to fill the school demand, report *most* favorable results.) For 1940, stores should be in a far better position to gauge the quantity they will need.
2. "Rudolph" gained momentum as it grew, last year . . . like a snowball rolling down-hill. This growing momentum will resume, next December, RIGHT WHERE IT LEFT OFF! The parents and children and teachers of your town will be *ready* for Rudolph, this year . . . rarin' to read it!

3. All comments from the stores, and from the management, lead us to believe that in "Rudolph" Wards has found a Christmas "natural"! A story that we can build up into a *nation-wide* Christmas institution, EXCLUSIVE WITH WARDS! (We have questioned a lot of children on the subject, and find that 95% of them infinitely prefer Rudolph to his 117-year-old predecessor, "The Night Before Christmas.")

4. "Rudolph" will receive far stronger promotion support in 1940 than it did in 1939:
   a. More newspaper advertising . . . (on the give-away book, as well as on the cloth-bound book and merchandise tie-ins we will SELL).
   b. A larger space in the Circular.
   c. A huge "Rudolph" background for every toy window.
   d. A more conspicuous interior display set-up.

5. We plan to complete our 1940 promotion of "Rudolph" by offering for sale, at full profit: —
   a. A cloth-bond edition of "Rudolph."
   b. A soft-toy Rudolph.
   c. A Rudolph toy-bank.
   d. A decorative figure of Rudolph, in china or glass.
   e. A nursery lamp, with "Rudolph" parchment shade.

. . . Because of these merchandise tie-ins, the *much*-stronger promotional support, and the huge momentum already built up . . . it is our opinion that there will be far more interest in "Rudolph" in 1940 than there was in 1939.[1]

Some managers may have found humor in the need to order extra books for school giveaways: in 1939, Ward's issued multiple warnings against giving away copies to any child without parents in tow.

There had been glitches with the plan to promote Rudolph in 1939. Even while many stores had run short of booklets, others had booklets left over from the previous year. This, perhaps, was no more than should have been expected from any organization with over six hundred individual stores, each with its own manager, to coordinate. Still, Ward's hoped that managers who had under-ordered *Rudolph* in 1939 had learned their lesson.

Montgomery Ward was clearly prepared for the second Rudolph campaign and had gone so far as to prepare mock-ups of store displays featuring Rudolph. By March, Ward's individual stores had filled out order slips for nearly one and a half million copies. By summer, however, something fundamental had changed. Preparations ground to a halt in August: the Rudolph promotion would be canceled. For some within the Ward's family, grounding Rudolph was a mistake. M. O. Boxwell wrote to H. E. MacDonald:

> I was very much surprised to receive your letter of August 6th advising that stores would not receive their commitment of "Rudolph, the Red-Nosed Reindeer."
>
> Frankly, Mac, I think this is a tremendous mistake. It is one of the little items that we had last year that I think caused more comment among our customers than anything promotional-wise we have ever done.
>
> Stores have made plans to distribute them to kindergartens and first-grade classes in the schools. As I remember, the cost was very reasonable, and I personally would recommend that, if necessary, we just deduct their cost from our newspaper advertising.
>
> But let's have "Rudolph"![2]

Why had Rudolph been grounded? Various reasons have been given, including paper shortages. Even as early as March 1940, a letter to store managers worried over printing costs. "The rising cost of paper makes it advisable that we take immediate steps regarding the printing of our give-away 'Rudolphs' for Christmas 1940. The price of paper has already gone-up considerably since we placed our 1939 order last fall."[3] It has also been suggested that Rudolph's name sounded too

Rudolph displays, Montgomery Ward, circa 1940 | Papers of Robert L. May, Rauner Special Collections Library, Dartmouth College; courtesy of Dartmouth College Library

German; but the United States would not enter the war until December 1941. Whatever the reason, however, there does not seem to be a letter or memo by a Ward's executive outlining specific issues.

Even as MacDonald issued the order to shelf Rudolph, he nonetheless expressed a personal interest in the red-nosed reindeer outside the business workday. In 1939 or 1940 he used Rudolph's image for two invitations, perhaps the first instance of the reindeer's image spilling over from his corporate gig. The first card, "Cheerio!," is an invitation to a gathering on Christmas day, and the cover shows an inebriated Rudolph with a drink in hand. As with the other posters for the Rudolph promotion, it would be interesting to know whether Denver Gillen also drew these. The second invitation shows a sober Rudolph for a less sober activity. At first, the invitation appears to have something to do with an official Ward's activity: a year-end wrap-up. On closer inspection, however, the "wrap-up" is a running gag, and the invitation seems to be for a stag party. In his off hours, the innocent Rudolph was growing up.

For May, it probably looked as though Rudolph would be permanently set aside by the more important concerns of the looming war. And why would Rudolph necessarily have a long shelf life as a promotional tool for Ward's? Most promotions came and went, making way for new ideas. For the next few years, Ward's remained embroiled in other problems that had little to do with Rudolph.

"Cheerio!," private Christmas party invitation and insert, circa 1940 | Papers of Robert L. May, Rauner Special Collections Library, Dartmouth College; courtesy of Dartmouth College Library

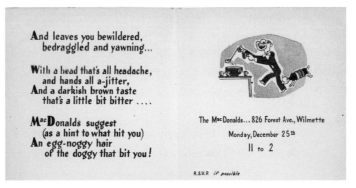

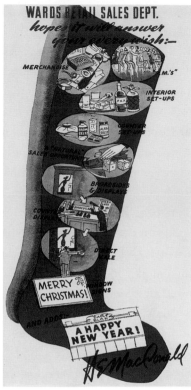

"Mr. MacDonald's X," cover and insert, circa 1940 | Papers of Robert L. May, Rauner Special Collections Library, Dartmouth College; courtesy of Dartmouth College Library

May, Rudolph, and World War II

While grounding Rudolph must have been a disappointment to May, he probably had plenty of other activities to occupy himself between 1940 and 1945. At the very beginning of this period, at least, he continued to be a single parent of a young child and an employee of Montgomery Ward. Barbara May later recalled:

> In the early 1940s, my father carpooled off to downtown Montgomery Wards from our Evanston apartment five mornings a week. On Saturday mornings—a standard part of the work week in those days—he'd drive

his own car, a 1941 coral-pink Buick, and sometimes I got to go with him. I felt pretty important as the daughter of the man who'd created Rudolph. Each weekday Dad prepared a floppy peanut-butter sandwich to eat in the car for breakfast on his way to Wards. I imagined him squinched into the car with four other men, chomping away, filling the tiny airspace with peanut butter fumes. I just hoped those other guys were partial to peanuts. All of dad's cars were in the red family, by the way. All General Motors cars—Buicks or Oldsmobiles—and all of them one shade or another of red.[4]

In 1940 May published another children's book, *Benny the Bunny Liked Beans*. While *Benny* would never reach canonical status like *Rudolph* (and indeed, even May's other *Rudolph* books never reached canonical status), *Kirkus Reviews* wrote, "Yes, it is comic supplement type of thing, with a bit of a moral—but it is fun, and it will serve a purpose of bridging over the child's interest from the funnies to books."[5]

During Rudolph's partial retirement, May could not help but notice the birth of a new competitor in 1942: Bambi. Perhaps Disney's interest in turning Felix Salten's book into a full-length movie helps explain the studio's noninterest in Rudolph: while one is a white-tailed deer and the other a reindeer, they look pretty much the same until Bambi grows up. *Bambi* started slowly, but as with many Disney films, it would be reintroduced periodically. Disney had been an innovator in cross-marketing and merchandising during the 1930s, basically mapping out how to develop and market a cartoon character. Later, in 1948, the "all

"Please, Mister, Don't Be Careless," United States Department of Agriculture, 1943

plush jumbo Bambi"[6] must have seemed very similar to the plush Rudolph that Ward's sold. Bambi's presence spread even further in 1943 and 1944 when he served as a spokes-animal for the Forest Service before Smokey Bear came along.

World War II brought big changes, both for May and Montgomery Ward. For May, the biggest change came on May 29, 1941, when he married Virginia Newton, also an employee of Ward's. Barbara, born in 1934, was soon joined by a growing family that included Joanna (born March 30, 1942) and Christopher Newton (March 5, 1943). Eventually, Virginia and Robert May would have three more children (Virginia in 1946, Martha in 1952, and Elizabeth Ann in 1958). In another letter to Dartmouth from 1946, May mentions his growing family of four children: "I'm afraid the resulting home-work will prevent my attending the 20th [an alumni event for the class of 1926]. By the way—does this [having four children] tie me for first in the class, or is there a '26 father-of-five?"[7] During these years, the May family remained living in an Evanston, Indiana, apartment.

May family Christmas card, circa 1940s | Papers of Robert L. May, Rauner Special Collections Library, Dartmouth College; courtesy of Dartmouth College Library

The changes at Montgomery Ward were equally large. Many believed that Sewell Avery had saved the company during the Depression, pushing for growth and producing larger profits during difficult times. Avery became more adversarial, however, when faced with the policies of President Roosevelt's National War Labor Board. These issues came to a head in 1944. Ward's refused to re-sign its contract with the United Mail Order, Warehouse and Retail Employees Union, setting off a strike. Roosevelt ordered both sides to cease, arguing that Montgomery Ward was essential to the delivery of farm equipment necessary for the war effort. The clash between Avery and the War Labor Board resulted in Roosevelt ordering the secretary of commerce to take over Ward's Chicago plant. On December 26, Avery still refused to comply, leading to his physical removal from Ward's property by an army sergeant and a private. Roosevelt issued a press statement:

> We cannot allow Montgomery Ward & Co. to set aside the wartime policies of the United States Government just because Mr. Sewell Avery does not approve of the Government's procedure for handling labor disputes. Montgomery Ward & Co., like every other corporation and every labor union in this country, has a responsibility to our fighting men. That responsibility is to see that nothing interferes with the continuity of our war production. It is because Montgomery Ward & Co. has failed to assume this obligation that I have been forced to sign an Executive Order directing the Secretary of War to take over and operate certain properties of Montgomery Ward & Co.[8]

With Ward's continued labor problems, the army seized the company's plants and facilities in Chicago, which remained under government control from December 28, 1944, to October 18, 1945.

Did these activities hurt Montgomery Ward as a business? This is an open question. In *The First Hundred Years Are the Toughest*, Cecil C. Hoge Sr. wrote: "Avery's struggles against the CIO [labor federation], the Army and the government were greatly sympathized with and applauded by many. Gradually, Avery was appearing more eccentric to more people. His success was so great and the position of Montgomery Ward was so strong that this eccentricity made him a conversation piece. However, he was diverting his energies and beginning to tie the arm of Ward behind its back for the post-war sprint about to start."[9] In the final consensus, Avery had been just the right man during the Depression but proved less capable during economic upturns.

The war, of course, affected everyone. For several years May helped direct the War Fund Drive in Chicago. May frequently wrote to Dartmouth, keeping the school up to date on his activities: "My only excuse for writing is to pass along the news that I was again asked to plan and write the advertising campaign for the annual Community and War Fund Drive of Greater Chicago."[10] For the drive, May designed advertisements that ran in Chicago papers, trade papers, and shopping news.[11] It was only in 1946, after the war came to an end, that May realized Rudolph might get a second chance: "Now that the 'duration' is over, we [Ward's] will again bring out 'Rudolph the Red-Nosed Reindeer' this Christmas . . . more than 2 million of them . . . to be distributed in all Wards 640 Retail Stores, and 200 Catalog Offices."[12]

Rudolph, after a partial retirement, was back in business.

Rudolph's Second Birthday

In 1946 Montgomery Ward geared up for a new Rudolph promotion, one that would rival the 1939 giveaway. While this promotion is less well documented than the one in 1939, Ward's strategy seems similar. Once again, Ward's contacted newspapers, emphasizing the novelty of the giveaway, along with the approval of teachers and psychologists. John Martin wrote: "We started receiving hundreds of requests from schools and libraries . . . even a request for 50 copies from the Chief Probation Officer of the Juvenile Court of Cook County (who apparently considered 'Rudolph' a good influence on bad children)."[13] Besides touching on the familiar talking points from 1939, Martin added that Cornelius Vanderbilt had "phoned to request copies on three separate trips through Chicago."[14] Other news included an attempt by the printer to buy the rights in order to publish a commercial version of *Rudolph*, along with overtures from a well-known Hollywood animator. Rudolph, Ward's assured, had lived up to his hype.

Martin also bragged about the number of copies that Ward's planned to distribute in 1946. Initially, the store estimated a print run of two million. When Ward's six-hundred-plus stores placed orders, however, the requested number of copies totaled nearly four million (3,800,700). Finally, Ward's ordered approximately three and a half million copies of *Rudolph* (3,476,000), reaching a total of 5,841,016 when combined with the 1939 copies (which has usually been rounded off to six million copies when discussing the giveaway totals from 1939 and 1946). Whereas Ward's had once emphasized *Rudolph*'s best-selling status and placed him within the tradition of *The Story of Ferdinand*, now his stock had risen: "We understand that this last figure puts 'Rudolph' way out in front of any 'best seller' on record . . . excepting only the Bible."[15] Rudolph, indeed, had joined illustrious company.

In regard to Ward's promotion during 1946, one small mystery remains. And like many good mysteries that date back sixty-five years, this one probably has no explanation. When Ward's decided to put Rudolph out to pasture in 1940, a surplus of books (left over from 1939) remained at a number of stores. In a report titled "1940 Orders for Give-Away Rudolphs," one note relayed, "35 stores stated that they had an adequate carryover from last year." (The report also noted that twenty-three stores "commented that a *new* story would have been a better idea.")[16] In other words, as Ward's geared up for the 1940 promotion that never took place, a number of copies of *Rudolph* remained under counters or in storage. The 2,365,000 copies of *Rudolph* "given" away in 1939 probably included these copies in storage. Since the thirty-five stores are not identified, we have no idea whether they were big or small stores. The number of stores, however, seems small within the total number of Ward's stores (620 in 1939). Still, there may have been thirty thousand or more copies of *Rudolph* that were never distributed. Furthermore, we have no idea why they were never distributed. It could be as simple as lack of demand, that the store had requested too many copies, or that the store somehow neglected to distribute the copies it had. While these numbers hardly affect the impressiveness of *Rudolph*'s initial mass distribution, it is nonetheless a curious bit of information.

What became of these extra copies of *Rudolph*? Possibly they were simply stored until after World War II and then distributed by Ward's in 1946. Still, the 1946 book *was* different from the 1939 book, though the difference was only something collectors of children's books might notice. The 1939 edition included a trimotor airplane on page nine; the 1946 edition has a four-motored plane.[17] Another possibility exists: these surplus copies were sacrificed to the war effort.

Stan Zielinski, in noting how only a "small portion of the two million giveaways have survived to today's collectible book market," touched indirectly on this possibility: "The original issue was in comic book-like format, with soft cover wraps. Giveaways being what giveaways be, most of the two million copies were read, read again and again, received wear, tear, torn covers, torn pages, then discarded, many copies serving their patriotic duty during the WWII paper drives."[18] It is rather unpleasant to think that surplus copies of *Rudolph* might have been simply discarded by the stores, even if for a good cause, though it would help explain the current cost of an original *Rudolph* from 1939: as of 2014, one copy at Abe Books was listed at $950. (The limited number of hardbacks, given away to Ward's executives in 1939, are even more valuable.)

While May must have been happy to see Rudolph make a comeback in 1946, the young reindeer's future was still very much in doubt. Seemingly, Ward's had little interest in developing Rudolph beyond the confines of retail products. May, however, believed that Rudolph had room to develop outside the Ward's family, and he also had an idea who could direct that growth: himself. Even so, his gaining the copyright for Rudolph, and the possibility of developing Rudolph outside of Ward's, remained distant possibilities in 1946. As long as Ward's held Rudolph's copyright, May's hands were tied.

Owning Rudolph

Another part of Rudolph's mythic story line focuses on the copyright being granted to Robert May at the beginning of 1947. Although May wrote *Rudolph*, he wrote it while employed by Montgomery Ward, which meant that Ward's owned the copyright to the book and anything marketed under the Rudolph trademark. It remains unclear when or how the subject of turning over the copyright to May was first introduced. Johnny Marks, May's brother-in-law and the author of the song "Rudolph the Red-Nosed Reindeer," later said that winning the copyright from Ward's had required lengthy litigation. "In the end, through a lot of trial and litigation, Bob got credit for his work and got it published."[19] This, however, seems to be the sole source referencing litigation. It is likely, however, that May—in some form—requested the copyright to *Rudolph* at some point between 1940 and 1946.

There were multiple reasons why May would have wanted the copyright. First, there seemed to be a great deal of interest in developing Rudolph beyond the original book. Even at Ward's in 1939 and 1940, many store managers suggested a number of products, partly in response to requests by customers. There also seemed to be a general belief by May and others that Rudolph could be transferred to other mediums, mainly animated shorts. While May clearly wanted to develop Rudolph in new directions, he needed one of two things to do so: either Ward's willingness to develop Rudolph along these lines within the company, or the transfer of the copyright, which would allow him to start his own company. While Ward's could have easily developed Rudolph as a toy (the company had plans to do so in 1940), the retail company seemed to have limited interest in the broader use of the reindeer's image.

At some point—probably during 1946—Ward's decided to give the copyright to May. May wrote about the possibility sometime in 1946: "Unless the management has a change of heart, Rudolph will then be released to me for personal publication and profit . . . with me in turn writing a new give-away for Wards for the following Christmas. So maybe in another few years, I'll be in this authoring business in a big way."[20] The note seems to imply an exchange between May and Ward's: May would write a new promotion (perhaps another promotion featuring Rudolph), and Ward's would turn over Rudolph's copyright. And seemingly May believed that Ward's retained the power to rescind its decision at this point (which probably meant May had never held a strong legal argument). Whether or not there were other agreements on the side (such as allowing Ward's to continue promoting and benefiting from Rudolph) remains unknown.

Extravagant motives have been given for the release of the copyright to May. In the *The Rudolph Factor*, Cyndi Laurin and Craig Morningstar wrote: "As it happened, he [May] was deeply in debt as a result of enormous medical expenses from his late wife's illness. In 1947, the CEO of Montgomery Ward, Sewell Avery, transferred the copyright to Robert May, and he and his daughter were able to reap the benefits of its success for several decades."[21] Stanley Frankel simply wrote that Avery was "touched by the beauty and simplicity of the Rudolph story, he ordered the copyright turned over to Bob—so that May could receive all royalties."[22] In December 1994, Tiffany J. Lewis wrote in *New Hampshire Premier*, "Montgomery Ward's staff lawyers wanted to retain the story's copyright for the company, but Chairman Sewell Avery overrode their objections and turned the copyright over to May in 1947."[23] Ace Collins interpreted the act as "one of the most generous decisions ever made by the head of a large company."[24] And Inez Whiteley Foster even suggests, in a *Christian Science Monitor* article from 1948, that after "realizing the tremendous merchandising possibilities of Rudolph's fast-growing popularity, in 1947 Montgomery Ward generously turned over copyright ownership to Author May so he might receive royalties."[25]

Together, these quotes leave the impression that the copyright issue evolved in the following way: May acquired debt because of his first wife's illness and death in the mid-to-late 1930s; the transfer of the copyright to May would help repay those debts, but some executives at Ward's objected to turning over a valuable asset; CEO Sewell Avery, touched by the story, overrode these objections, insisting that the copyright be given to May. Once this was done, May was able to repay his debts and, in some versions of the story, become wealthy.

To underline the simplicity of these accounts, one can turn to May's own version of the story from a 1975 *Guidepost* article. He offers the following narrative:

1. In 1947 a song publisher approached him about *Rudolph*.
2. May approached a company officer but was told that Ward's owned the copyright.
3. The matter was then brought up at a board meeting.
4. Avery decided that May should have the rights to *Rudolph*.

The last detail, in particular, offers a little drama. "Mr. Avery slapped his hand on the table and announced, 'I'm not interested in any reasons for our retaining the copyright. Let Bob May have it!'"[26]

May's narrative meshes well with the earlier details about Rudolph's origin, with Avery's selfless act mirroring Rudolph's own story. May, however, leaves out a number of points, including his own efforts to find commercial opportunities for Rudolph as early as 1939. There is a wonderful innocence to May's recollection: instead of fighting for the copyright or planning a business, he portrays everything about Rudolph as unfolding in the most natural way. There is no conflict or concern with money.

Avery's motivation may have been more pragmatic than having a big heart. Ward's clearly saw obstacles in developing Rudolph along certain lines. In a letter dated December 6, 1946, John Martin includes a footnote about the release of a recording of *Rudolph* (a spoken-word recording, to be made available by Victor Records in 1947): "To facilitate this recording, and any other perpetuation of 'Rudolph', Montgomery Ward released the complete copyright to the author, effective January 1, 1947."[27] Even as the company turned over the copyright, however, it continued to market and promote Rudolph. Ward's included, for instance, Rudolph-related toys in its catalog. Likewise, Ward's would be involved in other promotional schemes with Rudolph in 1947, after the copyright had already been turned over to May. Ward's, it seems, had the best of both worlds, being seen as generously granting the copyright to May while continuing to make use of Rudolph for promotion and profit.

There is one other source of insight concerning the release of the copyright. National Public Radio spoke with Barbara May Lewis in 2013. Lewis said that Ward's never viewed Rudolph as having a life outside of a Christmas promotion for the store. "They didn't know," Lewis told NPR. "They didn't know. It was just this silly little almost booklet."[28] With this observation, it might be suggested that Ward's release of the copyright was less an example of corporate kindness than the simple relinquishing of an asset that was quickly losing value as a promotional tool.

Rudolph would continue to be promoted by Montgomery Ward during the mid-to-late 1940s, with free books giving way to other knickknacks. Over time, however, Rudolph became less central to the retail giant's seasonal sales, taking his place as a toy among many other toys in the company's catalog. Promotional excitement built on novelty had a limited shelf life: one seasonal promotion, in the long run, made room for another. In the life of most promotional characters, this would have been the end of the road. For Rudolph and May, it only proved a new beginning.

four

RUDOLPH MERCHANDISE
AND THE BABY BOOM

If 1946 was a big year for Rudolph, Ward's and May believed that 1947 could be even bigger. "Meet Rudolph the Red-Nosed Reindeer," a *Chicago Daily Tribune* advertisement shouted, and "follow the lead of Santa's new leader to Wards!"[1] While no one could guess the long-term interest in Santa's new star, Ward's planned to promote Rudolph aggressively in 1947–48 and perhaps beyond. Wishing to avoid earlier mistakes, Ward's metamorphosed Rudolph from a character in a book to a line of merchandise. In 1947 young boys or girls could own a seventeen-inch Rudolph stuffed toy along with a new version (with new art) of May's original book; in 1948 they could see an animated Rudolph cartoon at local theaters. As the holiday season of 1947 opened, Rudolph was flying high and aiming even higher.

While no one would have called it good luck in 1940, the delays caused by World War II probably worked in Robert L. May and his progeny Rudolph's favor. The three and a half million copies of the book given away in 1946 would have introduced Rudolph to a different set of children. But this was only the beginning. When Rudolph was reintroduced by Ward's as a giveaway in 1946, the young reindeer's rebirth mirrored the birth of the biggest generation thus far in American history: the baby boom.

The term itself—baby boom—has become so familiar that we have lost the historical import of this massive influx of children on American culture and its economy. "In the two decades following World War II," wrote LeRoy Ashby, "the baby boom resulted in 80 million births, almost 40 percent of the U.S. population."[2] In part, the very expansion of postwar America depended on new consumers—including small ones—to keep the country growing. In the suburbs, parents needed bigger cars and larger houses for three- and four-child families; and within suburban homes, even the basics—food and clothing—would spur massive industry growth. Beyond the basics, children under twelve became a market unto themselves for a cornucopia of toys, games, and anything tied to the latest trend. And Christmas promised to be the biggest bonanza of all.

While Rudolph never seemed to get much older, a generation of babies— described over time as war babies, the Pepsi Generation, Spock babies, and the me generation—would grow up with him. In fact, they would never be able to remember a time when Rudolph had failed to serve as Santa's right-hand reindeer. Rudolph, like Santa, the other eight reindeer, and a hundred years of holiday folklore, was no more or less than the sum total of an American child's Christmas.[3]

In 1947–48 both May and Ward's began to tap into this budding market. During this time the relationship between Ward's and May—in regard to Rudolph—remained central. Ward's promoted Rudolph heavily in both years and reserved catalog space for Rudolph merchandise. Ward's provided the funds for a Rudolph giveaway (a three-dimensional punch-out) in 1947 and for an animated cartoon in 1948. May now owned Rudolph, allowing him to license the image for games and toys, but Ward's continued to exploit Rudolph each Christmas season. Together, May and Ward's tested the waters for the postwar boom and Rudolph's future.

Rudolph the Red-Nosed Reindeer Enterprises Inc.

On January 1, 1947, the copyright for "Rudolph the Red-Nosed Reindeer" was transferred to Robert L. May. Now May would be free to develop Rudolph along a number of commercial paths that had been suggested since the end of 1939. Whether May envisioned Rudolph as a commercial book, an animated color cartoon, or a toy line, the market in postwar America seemed wide open. Since licensing for toys had become a big market during the slow Depression years (Shirley Temple dolls, for instance), neither May nor Ward's had to reinvent the wheel. The possibilities must have seemed promising to May, even overwhelming: now, after eight years of waiting, Rudolph could wander out into the wider world. "All very exciting," May noted in a letter, "to the point of being scarcely believable."[4]

Even by the middle of 1947, May had a large number of projects either in progress or about to be realized. He wrote a long letter to Charles Widmayer at Dartmouth in August, outlining many of them:

1. An RCA Victor record album narrated by Paul Wing, special music composed by George Kleinsinger
2. A deluxe edition of the Rudolph book, with new and greatly improved artwork
3. A big Rudolph "stuffed toy" (seventeen inches tall) manufactured by the Ideal Toy and Novelty Company
4. A box of three Rudolph picture-puzzles
5. A sterling silver Rudolph charm
6. Rudolph slippers for children
7. Rudolph sweatshirts for children
8. Rudolph T-shirts for children[5]

And May was just getting warmed up. Rudolph was also on his way to becoming a theatrical cartoon, a Parker Brothers game ("the game where every child can be Santa Claus"), and a flashlight—among many other potential projects.[6]

Despite the copyright change, however, Montgomery Ward remained heavily involved in all things Rudolph. "Needless to say," May wrote of the many projects, "Montgomery Ward is capitalizing on the opportunity to sell these Rudolph products."[7] This capitalization would include two color pages in the new Ward's Christmas catalog, along with a number of exclusives: "The promotion will be similarly featured in the ads, circulars, windows, and interior displays of Wards

631 stores . . . and by Wards 230 catalog offices. In addition, all these stores and offices will advertise and distribute free this Christmas a new type of Rudolph give-away."[8] May also continued working for Ward's, leaving little gap between promoting Rudolph at work and at home.

In December 1947 Ward's issued a full-page ad with Rudolph dramatically sweeping across the sky, leading the way with the other eight reindeer and Santa close behind:

> Maybe you've met him already . . . the poor little deer with the big, shiny nose that saved the day for Santa, one extra-foggy Christmas Eve. Millions of children have heard his story . . . *first* told by Wards, then recorded by RCA Victor. Rudolph today is famous. (He'll soon be in the *movies*, even!) But he still makes Montgomery Ward his Christmas headquarters. He's learned, in his travels with Santa, that you just can't beat Wards for Christmas shopping . . . the *easy* way, the *thrifty* way! Come in and meet Rudolph, at Wards. And when you come in, bring your gift-list along. You'll find that Wards wide assortments include the answer to each of your Christmas problems. And that Wards thrifty pricing, time after time, permits you to buy A BETTER GIFT FOR THE PRICE YOU PLANNED TO PAY![9]

On top of his duties with Santa, then, Rudolph also worked as a holiday sales-deer for Ward's.

The promotion included another mass giveaway, this time a toy reindeer that could be pieced together to form a three-dimensional Rudolph. "They remove it from the envelope," wrote the *St. Petersburg Times*, "push out the pieces, assemble them, play with the deer, then take it apart, replace each piece in its proper niche in the board, slip it back in the envelope—and start all over again."[10] The envelope included the following message: "When you get home . . . bring Rudolph the Red-Nosed Reindeer to life by pushing-out the pieces of the puzzle, and fitting them together snugly . . . When you're through playing with Rudolph, take the pieces apart, put them back in the holes . . . then 'back to bed' in this envelope,

*Glow comes from mouth. Red
nose is transparent plastic
and glows when light is on.
Tail is moved to switch on
light.*

3400

Job #40-165   " Rudolph" Flashlight

Rudolph flashlight |
Montgomery Ward
Collection, Box 44,
Folder 3, American
Heritage Center, Uni-
versity of Wyoming

till you're ready to play Rudolph again. This Rudolph the Red-Nose Reindeer is
Yours . . . with Christmas Greetings from Montgomery Ward."[11] As often happened
with free promotions, other Rudolph products were advertised on the back of the
envelope, including a deluxe version of the book, the RCA recording, slippers, a
box of three puzzles, a fifteen-inch stuffed Rudolph, and a sweatshirt.[12]

Several toys offered a clue regarding the age market that May and Ward's were
targeting.

First there was the Rudolph flashlight, which depicted Rudolph in a kneeling
position. A description of the product was offered as follows: "Glow comes from
mouth. Red nose is transparent plastic and glows when light is on. Tail is moved
to switch on light."[13] For the Rudolph lamp, a mold of the reindeer served as the
base, while a lampshade was decorated with pictures of the young reindeer sleeping

Rudolph lamp |
Montgomery Ward
Collection, Box 44,
Folder 3, American
Heritage Center, Uni-
versity of Wyoming

Rudolph school
bag | Montgomery
Ward Collection,
Box 44, Folder 3,
American Heritage
Center, University
of Wyoming

on a pillow, riding on skis, and reading an "ABC" book. A stuffed Rudolph was described as "soft; lifelike; lovable! Plush coat, red nose, rolling eyes! 17 inches tall! Very low priced!"[14] And there is a school bag, featuring twin sets of Rudolph (head profiles) on one side and a picture of a dashing Rudolph on the other. Clearly all of these products were aimed at young children, the same age group that either read *Rudolph* or had *Rudolph* read to them.

One newspaper ad from the *Milwaukee Journal* in 1950 helps show how a Rudolph flashlight ($1) and bank ($1.25) were marketed: "Any child will tell you . . . toys that work are more fun. That's why they'll love little Rudolph the red nosed reindeer in a flashlight or a coin bank. With every coin deposit Rudolph's bright red nose flashes a friendly acknowledgement. The beam of light in the flashlight comes from Rudolph's nose . . . just press down on the tail and it lights. It's ideal for your child's bedside."[15] The ad is clearly aimed at adults buying for small children, a tactic that may have even seemed old-fashioned by 1950. The other oddity in this particular ad is the date: April 5. While Rudolph merchandise seemed best suited for the Christmas season, some items apparently were sold year-round.

This approach to developing Rudolph, however, was not always uniform. At one point, a company manufactured a set of tumbler glasses featuring Rudolph. While children could have used these for everyday drinking glasses, they seemed designed for highballs (May refers to the tumblers in a letter as "Rudolph highball glasses"[16]). It is difficult now, without having access to the original plans for the product, to understand the designated market for a package of eight highball glasses with a picture of Rudolph. This was the type of image confusion that Disney avoided when turning down an opportunity to put Mickey Mouse on an ashtray.[17]

A hardback book in 1947 was another part of Rudolph's promotion. But while a new edition of *Rudolph* may have seemed a natural development, it could have easily never happened. In 1947 *Rudolph* as a book had one tremendous handicap: Montgomery Ward had given away three and a half million copies the year before. Now a book publisher would be asking parents to *pay* for a new copy, and how many children would even need one? The market for a new book, then, may have seemed unpromising or, in the best-case scenario, fairly small.

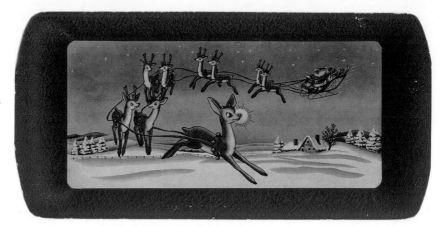

Harry Elbaum of the Maxton Publishers nonetheless took a chance. "All my life I've been kidded about my own nose," Elbaum later said, "so Rudolph won my sympathy from the start."[18] The hardback *Rudolph* (7¼ by 10¼ inches) would sell for fifty cents a copy. In a promotional sheet for the book, Maxton asserts that children now prefer *Rudolph* to all other Christmas stories: "Impartial tests by teachers, parents and psychologists show that 9 of every 10 children prefer 'RUDOLPH' to *any other Christmas story!* 'RUDOLPH' has all the magic Santa Claus appeal of 'The Night Before Christmas' . . . plus humor, action and a lovable young animal hero."[19] The real surprise, perhaps, was how quickly copies sold. Despite the mass giveaway in 1946, Maxton printed and sold 100,000 copies in 1947. "It wasn't enough—not nearly enough," wrote William Bentley in the *Chicago Sunday Times*.[20] The following year, the company would print 250,000 copies.

One development with the new edition of the book would continue over time: *Rudolph*'s history would be rearranged and, on occasion, erased. In 1947, Denver Gillen's illustrations would be replaced by Marion Guild's. In fact, while Gillen has often been credited as a key player in the book's initial success (his drawings helped sell the Rudolph idea to May's boss), he never seemed to hold any share of the copyright. All the future illustrators of Rudolph would clearly be guns for hire, while even May's poem, in the 1958 Little Golden Books version of *Rudolph*, would be replaced by Barbara Shook Hazen's prose. May's idea would be all that remained of the original, and this would become even more pronounced after the success of Rankin/Bass's animated special in 1964.

One other prominent product at the time was a set of four records with a music-accompanied reading of the *Rudolph* story in 1947. At the time, 78 rpm records remained the dominant form (though both the 33⅓ rpm format in 1948 and the 45 rpm format in 1949 challenged the 78 rpm) and had the capacity for approximately three minutes per side. For a twelve-minute rendition of *Rudolph* by Paul Wing, then, RCA put together a package of two records, each with A and B sides. RCA was optimistic: "An immediately outstanding success, the RCA Victor recording of 'RUDOLPH THE RED-NOSED REINDEER' shows promise of becoming a juvenile counterpart of 'White Christmas'—Nationwide advertising. An album of 2 unbreakable records . . . narrated by PAUL WING with musical score by GEORGE KLEINSINGER."[21] May noted that "it will be extensively advertised by Victor; sold by all the thousands of Victor outlets."[22]

Even though May's "to do" list must have seemed filled with Rudolph, he managed to write a third children's book, *Winking Willie*, in 1948 (*Benny the Bunny Liked Beans* was published in 1940). The new book was also published by Maxton. Reviewing the book, *Dartmouth Alumni Magazine* wrote, "*Winking Willie* is the familiar story of the social pariah, in this instance about a little dog with an outsize tail."[23] Here, May seemed to be working in a familiar niche.

Max Fleischer and Jam Handy

For a project that reached millions of viewers in 1948 and 1949 in movie theaters, the first animated *Rudolph the Red-Nosed Reindeer* has left few historical traces. While the nine-minute Max Fleischer cartoon is easily available to anyone with an Internet connection (the cartoon has fallen into public domain), the original version—without the familiar song at the beginning—has been a rarity until recently. Perhaps one of the most curious facts about the cartoon is that com-

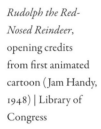

*Rudolph the Red-
Nosed Reindeer,*
opening credits
from first animated
cartoon (Jam Handy,
1948) | Library of
Congress

mentators cannot seem to agree on the date: many write 1944, others 1948. And
finally, while the earliest animated version of *Rudolph* remains charming, it seems
to have been superseded in the public's mind by the 1964 Rankin/Bass special.

Like the accounts that circulate about Robert May and the creation of *Rudolph*
in 1939, descriptions of the Fleischer cartoon are equally confusing and often inac-
curate. On the Internet and in print, the cartoon is frequently dated to 1944. Some
sources suggest that it was not shown in 1944 (because of the war), while others
note only that the original did not include the song (Johnny Marks's "Rudolph
the Red-Nosed Reindeer"). One version, rather fantastically, even states that the
song and music were included in the 1944 version, offering a framework for the
Gene Autry single in 1949. Many of these sources also mention a revival of the
cartoon in 1948 or 1949 with the addition of a song, based on Marks's written
music and Autry's popular version. The oddity of these stories for a researcher is

twofold: not only are the dates wrong, but many of these accounts contain more inaccuracies than accuracies.

The idea of taking Rudolph from book form to the animated screen dated as far back as 1939. May made inquiries, and friends—in letters—thought that Rudolph would be a natural for a studio like Disney. Even though *Rudolph* could reach millions through Montgomery Ward giveaways, an animated cartoon with a wide release could reach many more people. Irving S. Heineman Jr., writing to May at the beginning of 1940, noted, "Fifty Million people a week see our [Looney Tunes and Merrie Melodies] cartoons."[24] Multiple issues, however, got in the way. If Ward's owned the copyright, a cartoon version of *Rudolph* could be construed as no more than a commercial. Heineman wrote, "Would we be able to use the book without paying a royalty for its use[?] Would Montgomery Ward have to be given screen credit[?]"[25] With the war, the project, along with Rudolph, was put aside for another day.

May and Ward's, however, seemed less worried than Heineman about conflicts of interest. The *Rudolph* cartoon would be commissioned with financing provided by Montgomery Ward, even though it was May who now owned the copyright to Rudolph. This, perhaps, is one of the reasons that many people have misdated the cartoon to 1944. The original version of the cartoon opened with a plug for the retail giant: "Christmas Greetings from Montgomery Ward."[26] This may have given the impression that the cartoon had been made when Ward's still held the copyright. Even as May introduced Rudolph to the wider world, then, the red-nosed reindeer remained corralled at Ward's throughout the holiday season.

In 1948 Ward's promoted the *Rudolph* cartoon heavily with multiple newspaper ads: "See the great movie of Rudolph The Red-Nosed Reindeer! . . . Wards' famous Christmas story . . . now a classic! The touching tale of the funny-face deer who made good with Santa! Charmingly directed by MAX FLEISCHER himself! Narrated by Victor's famous PAUL WING . . . with a background of beautiful Christmas music."[27] Below the promotion Ward's included an advertisement for Rudolph gifts, including a flashing-nose bank and "a FREE Rudolph, too!

*Rudolph the Red-
Nosed Reindeer*
(Jam Handy, 1948) |
Library of Congress

. . . A Magic-Toy Rudolph whose shiny red nose really lights-up the darkness."[28] Another ad noted, "The Santa Claus movie every child has been waiting for! Don't miss it!"[29]

Another reason the dates are frequently confused is that the cartoon was altered in 1951 to include a version of "Rudolph the Red-Nosed Reindeer" with a choral arrangement by Harry R. Wilson. Since the original version of the cartoon did not include a song, the song would have had to be grafted onto hundreds of copies for release in movie theaters. "Rudolph the Red-Nosed Reindeer" may have been written by Johnny Marks as early as 1948 (not 1944), but it only became publicly known when Gene Autry's version became a hit in the winter of 1949. As such, it would have been too late to graft the song onto the movie in 1949. It appears that at some point after 1949 (probably in 1951), Johnny Marks bought the film from Ward's or Jam Handy and had the changes made. When the changes were made, Ward's sponsorship was erased from the film.

In regard to dating the movie, May mentions it in an August 29, 1947, letter to Charles Widmayer at Dartmouth: "Rudolph has gone to *Hollywood*, too! An animated sound movie in Technicolor . . . Max Fleischer direction; Paul Wing narration . . . will be shown in the theaters next Christmas season, sponsored by Montgomery Ward, in all the 861 cities and towns where Wards have made Rudolph famous. In the lobbies of these theaters will be counter displays or posters advertising the Rudolph merchandise. It is Wards belief that the showing of this Rudolph movie can be successfully repeated for many years to come."[30] Earlier in 1947, the *Dartmouth Alumni Magazine* simply noted that "Hollywood is shuffling eagerly on the outskirts of the crowd with ideas about cartooning Rudolph."[31] The discrepancy over the release date of the animated *Rudolph* can also be cleared up in the pages of *Billboard*. In its December 17, 1949, issue, *Billboard* noted that the Fleischer cartoon had been made the previous year.[32]

The *Rudolph* cartoon was commissioned by Montgomery Ward, perhaps in 1947. May mentions only the *possibility* of a cartoon at the beginning of 1947; by August, however, the cartoon seems to be in progress. Basically, Ward's had hired a studio—as opposed to a studio paying Ward's or May to produce a Rudolph cartoon—to make the animated short. Ward's chose the Jam Handy Organization, a filmmaking outfit located in Detroit. Handy's studio made training and promotional films for companies like General Motors and Coronet Instructional (an offshoot of *Coronet* magazine). At the time, Max Fleischer, famous for *Betty Boop* and *Popeye*, sat at the head of Jam Handy.

One aspect of the 1948 *Rudolph* that stands out today is how closely the nearly nine-minute cartoon mirrors May's original story. Or, as May would later write, "98% of the words are directly from my original 'poem' . . . with none of the gadgetry and extras that are in the TV Special."[33] Because the cartoon follows May's text so closely, the animation can give the impression of bringing the book to life. As the story begins, reindeer slide on the ice, protected by pillows, and decorate pine trees. The good-natured Rudolph tries to join in the fun, attaching a pillow, but the other reindeer remove it and ridicule the young buck: "Go on home red-nose, your Mama's calling you"[34] (certainly not from the original book).

*Rudolph the Red-
Nosed Reindeer*
(Jam Handy,
1948) | Library of
Congress

Rudolph's mom, who never speaks in the book, cheers him up, reminding him that "tonight you hang up your stocking."[35] As in May's books, the reindeer behave much like humans, walking on two legs, talking, and living in snug houses and sleeping in beds.

The fog, of course, leads to the same difficulties for Santa Claus, with the reindeer becoming entangled in tree branches and nearly crashing into an airplane. Only when Santa delivers presents to Rudolph's room, a room lit by a mysterious source, does he discover the solution to his problem: Rudolph, with his red nose, must lead the sleigh. Rudolph, after writing a note to his mom and dad ("Deer Mommy and Daddy"[36]), joins Santa's team. Even before the evening is through, Rudolph's fame spreads to all the other reindeer. As the head of Santa's team, Rudolph becomes the most famous and beloved reindeer of all.

Fleischer's *Rudolph* is quite charming, and if it possesses a flaw it is simply this: the cartoon seems to be over before it starts. For those familiar with more contemporary Christmas specials, running between twenty-five and fifty minutes,

*Rudolph the Red-
Nosed Reindeer*
(Jam Handy,
1948) | Library of
Congress

Rudolph the Red-Nosed Reindeer (Jam Handy, 1948) | Library of Congress

Rudolph the Red-Nosed Reindeer, from closing credits (Jam Handy, 1948) | Library of Congress

this probably seems like a letdown. For audiences in 1948 and 1949, however, this short would have been the perfect length for pre-feature fare. It would have also matched what audiences already knew about both May's book and Johnny Marks's song. Brightly lit by Technicolor and narrated by Paul Wing, *Rudolph* opened nationwide in the winter of 1948.

Rudolph and the Baby Boom

A number of articles in the late 1950s noted May's growing family and, often, the jealousy incited by May's first son: Rudolph. May, it seems, had been in the habit of discussing Rudolph-related business at the supper table after work. May told the *Chicago Daily Tribune*, "I talked so much about Rudolph at the supper table that there wasn't time for the children to tell about the more important things that happened to them during the day. So they voted in a family ordinance forbidding me to talk about Rudolph until after their bedtime."[37] At the time of the *Daily Tribune* article in 1950, Robert and Virginia May were photographed with four children: Barbara, sixteen; Joanna, nine; Christopher, eight; and Ginger, five. While none of the children qualified as baby boomers (they had all been born before 1946), the May family nonetheless mirrored the burgeoning trend.

Ward's and May's reintroduction of Rudolph in 1946 proved perfect timing: Rudolph would grow up with the biggest wave of new children the country had ever seen. The postwar economy supported and benefited from this trend, providing the money needed to raise a greater number of children *and* eventually selling products to and for these children. In enlarging itself as a country, America also ensured an expansive in-house market. These trends merged in the preteen market, clarifying the idea that children could also be viewed as consumers and that advertisers could ignore the parents and reach children directly. This trend ratcheted up even higher during the postwar-Christmas season, promising a smorgasbord of dolls, toys, and games.

While the baby boom is often fixed between 1946 and 1964, the national birthrate (preceded by the marriage rate) began spiking as early as 1943. Since the boom followed the lower birthrates of the 1920s and 1930s, it proved even more impressive. During the Depression years (1929–41) many Americans delayed marriage, while those who were married had fewer children. With the end of World War II, Americans quickly made up for lost time: in 1947 returning soldiers and fresh suburbanites set a record high, giving birth to 3.8 million children.[38]

At the time, however, many critics believed that the boom was temporary. After Americans had made up for lost time, the reasoning went, the birthrate would settle down to the zero-growth trend of recent decades. Instead, the growth rate exploded for nineteen years (1946–64). "The fertility rate rose 50 percent from 1940 to 1957," noted Steven Mintz and Susan Kellogg, "producing a population growth rate approaching that of India."[39] This growth reached an all-time high in 1957: every second, a child was born.[40] "In the two decades following World War II," noted LeRoy Ashby, "the baby boom resulted in 80 million births, almost 40 percent of the U.S. population."[41] As a result, the median age of the American population became increasingly younger.

The booming population worked hand in hand with a booming economy. When the war came to a close in the summer of 1945, the United States was more than victorious: it was a world power. While many European countries worked hard to rebuild from the devastation of war, America's industrial production emerged from the conflict unscathed. Factories switched from war to domestic production, filling suburban homes with furniture and appliances. And while economic forecasters fretted that the expansion would be short-lived—that the economy might slip back into another depression—this never happened. These worries, however, spurred efforts to keep consumption high. "By buying products," Ashby wrote, "consumers not only prevented another depression but also demonstrated the economic vitality and appeal of the United States."[42] Consumption and patriotism went hand in hand.

Both booms altered markets forever. While the economically independent teenager may have been discovered in the mid-1940s, marketing to the preteen became a growing trend for manufacturers during these postwar years. "More than 55.77 million children were under fifteen years old in 1960," noted Gary

Robert May and
Rudolph (date
unknown) | Papers
of Robert L. May,
Rauner Special Col-
lections Library, Dart-
mouth College; cour-
tesy of Dartmouth
College Library

Cross, "compared to only 32.97 million in 1940."[43] Cross continues: "The U.S. was also entering an unprecedented period of prosperity, allowing the parents of the baby boom generation to spend far more on playthings than their parents had. Affluence opened purse strings to the wishes of the young for the novelties of play."[44] There were certain anxieties associated with an expanding market. If toy makers produced too many toys, the items simply remained in the warehouse; if department stores stocked too many toys, these items became an inventory surplus.[45] Nevertheless, despite all of Ward's plans in 1947, there were still shortages of Rudolph products. The opportunity was immense, and toy makers responded. "Toy manufactures and other amusement businesses," noted Ashby, "scrambled eagerly to cash in on the surging baby-boomer market."[46]

All trends merged at Christmas, the real jackpot for toy makers and baby boomers. As early as the 1820s, an American Christmas began focusing on these two things: children and gifts. The domestic Christmas *and* the consumer Christmas, then, were intertwined from the very start. When Moore introduced "A Visit from St. Nicholas" in the 1820s, an Americanized Santa Claus served as a binding symbol: parents had permission to spend lavishly on their children without guilt. Santa, after all, delivered the goods. Following the Civil War, these gifts would increasingly be store-bought. All these trends would accelerate following World War II, thanks to an even greater focus on a child-centered Christmas. Susan Waggoner observed: "To anyone who wasn't part of the baby boom generation, it's almost impossible to convey the sheer pleasure of finding yourself in the center of a world in which you were, well, the center of the world. Never was a generation so eager to indulge its children as the fathers and mothers who'd grown up during a depression and matriculated into a war, and the huge volume of children born between 1945 and 1964 created a class of tiny consumers who wielded staggering power at the checkout line."[47] The bonanza for this new market arrived once a year every year at Christmas, making Rudolph a very valuable commodity.

Rudolph Redux

Fleischer's *Rudolph* would also be widely seen in 1949. That year, *Billboard* reported that Montgomery Ward delivered three hundred copies of the cartoon to Times-Columbia, a distributor. Indeed, Ward's handed over the national promotional rights to *Rudolph*, and the copies were delivered free of charge. Arthur Keen of Time-Columbia cut a deal with RKO, allowing *Rudolph* to run simultaneously in its thirty-seven theaters, while the remaining copies "will blanket the Eastern States."[48] To promote the cartoon, "sixty thousand *Rudolph* balloons, each with the name of the local shop, are to be given away free to kids attending the theater."[49] There were also contests with prizes provided by the companies that made Rudolph products. When New York City's Gertz's Department Store tried to take advantage of Rudolph-mania by creating a talking reindeer, Montgomery Ward countered by borrowing a live deer from the local zoo.

What was unknown to May during these years was how long Rudolph's high-charting flight would last. In one article in the *New York Herald Tribune*, May compared the Rudolph phenomenon to an oil well. "The well may keep on gushing or it may ease off to a trickle. Right now it looks as if Rudolph will take care of us."[50]

A couple of points are worth mentioning in relation to Rudolph's longevity. In 1948 no one knew that Rudolph would go down in history. Even while Rudolph was warmly embraced by American children in 1939 and again directly after World War II, he had received massive amounts of promotion from the second-most-powerful retailer in the United States. Robert May rode this wave. In the winter of 1948, however, May had only owned the trademark to Rudolph for less than two years. While the toy line may have been promising and the promotional cartoon a success, Rudolph—at this point in his life—still qualified as a fad. Even the monetary success of Rudolph in 1947–48 would have been difficult to measure. Ward's obviously felt the promotion worthwhile, but May continued to work at the company as he promoted his progeny on the side. Rudolph nonetheless had one advantage that even Mickey Mouse lacked: he was associated with Santa Claus and Christmas. If Ward's, May, and others could permanently tie Rudolph to America's Yuletide holiday tradition, he would be on his way to becoming a folk icon.

five

JOHNNY MARKS,
GENE AUTRY, AND
"RUDOLPH THE
RED-NOSED REINDEER"

During the latter half of the 1940s, Rudolph lived a charmed life. Translated to every form of media and instrument of child's play, he easily segued from spoken-word records to cartoons and toys. At each step, he reached a new segment of his baby-boom fan base. In 1946, after a seven-year hiatus, Ward's threw Rudolph a grand party to reintroduce him to American children. This prepped millions of kids for the new edition of *Rudolph* issued by Maxton in 1947, followed by Max Fleischer's color cartoon of the red-nosed reindeer in the winter of 1948. As the fortunes of Mickey, Porky, and Popeye ebbed and flowed, Rudolph offered the promise of outgrowing his fad status and becoming a permanent feature on the American Christmas scene. His association with Christmas was his greatest asset but also his greatest liability: for ten months of the year he disappeared, and no one knew what the next holiday would hold. In newspaper interviews, Robert May sometimes offered a realistic assessment of all things Rudolph: yes, he was very popular *now*, but who knew how long it would last?

At no time was the young deer's life more charmed than when Johnny Marks wrote, and Gene Autry sang, "Rudolph the Red-Nosed Reindeer" in 1949. Robert May guessed that a song could make Rudolph more popular; it is doubtful he imagined *how* popular. Writing a song about Rudolph was an old idea, one among many that May had for promoting the young buck. Like the cartoon, however, it was an idea that sat on the back shelf until Ward's turned Rudolph's copyright over to May in 1947. Even then, wanting a song and getting one were two different things.

The animated *Rudolph* may have underlined the need for a theme song: in the cartoon, the musical score simply relies on familiar Christmas carols and songs. Despite the need for the song, the idea would not come to fruition until after the animated *Rudolph* had been released. It seems likely that May began to pursue this possibility more seriously in 1948–49, perhaps considering several songwriters before settling on Johnny Marks. Marks had two advantages: he was already an established songwriter, and he was married to May's sister, Margaret.

One of the stickiest issues when looking at "Rudolph the Red-Nosed Reindeer," however, is that of copyright. Marks seems to have maintained most of the copyright of "Rudolph" as a song, meaning that he was the primary beneficiary of the song's royalties over the years. The issue of who held the song's copyright was probably decided by May and Marks early on; without May's permission to write a song, Marks presumably could have been sued. Marks's foresight in forming St. Nicholas Music to publish "Rudolph" further guaranteed that he kept most of the profits; if he had registered "Rudolph" with another music publisher, he would have had to split the royalties.

It is doubtful that May, or even Marks, realized just *how* long the song would remain popular and *how* much the song alone would be worth. Both May's permission to write the song and Marks's primary ownership of the song, however, must have created a legal quagmire: two people, May and Marks, now had legal claims over different aspects of Rudolph. Marks's apparently uncontested copyright of the song may have also set a precedent for future Rudolph-related projects: while May granted permission for "Rudolph," Marks could probably pen his next Rudolph song of his own accord. While Marks promoted "Rudolph" and other songs that he penned for St. Nicholas Music, Rudolph the Red-Nosed Reindeer Enterprises focused on toys and licensing opportunities.

Johnny Marks, "Rudolph the Red-Nosed Reindeer," sheet music, circa 1949 | Papers of Robert L. May, Rauner Special Collections Library, Dartmouth College; courtesy of Dartmouth College Library

Back in the Saddle Again

Gene Autry offered the standard version of the "Rudolph" story in his 1978 mem-
oir, *Back in the Saddle Again*, and this would be the version most often repeated
by him and many others writing about the song. Following the success of "Here
Comes Santa Claus" in 1947–48 (first with Autry's version, followed by a number
of others), Autry was in the market for a new Christmas song. He had identified
three songs that he liked, "He's a Chubby Little Fellow," "Santa, Santa, Santa," and
"If It Doesn't Snow on Christmas," for the upcoming recording session. Normally,
however, each session covered four songs, leaving Autry one short. He wrote:
"Meanwhile, a young New York songwriter named Johnny Marks had mailed me
a home recording of a number called 'Rudolph the Red-nosed Reindeer.' I played
it at home that night for my wife. It not only struck me as silly but I took the
position that there were already too many reindeer flying around."[1] Ina, Autry's
wife, felt differently. "Oh Gene, it reminds me of the story of the Ugly Duckling.
I think you ought to give it a try. The kids will love it."[2]

While Autry remained unconvinced, he was running out of time. He passed
the home recording along to Carl Cotner, his musical director, with a shrug of his
shoulders: "After all, we still have to do four songs."[3] The recording session itself,
held in the middle of the summer, was a rocky one. After they struggled through
the first three songs, Cotner told Autry, "Gene, we have less than ten minutes left.
What do you want to do?" Autry glanced at the clock and answered, "It's only
that 'Rudolph' thing. Throw it in and let's go."[4] Despite the successful one-take of
"Rudolph," no one was sure that the recording would ever be used for more than
a B side. When Autry performed the song at a live show in September, however,
something special happened: "America fell in love with the red-nosed reindeer. I
introduced the song that winter in Madison Square Garden, at the annual rodeo
we did there. We had a guy dressed in a reindeer costume with a big bulb of a nose,
and when I got to the second verse of the song they threw a blue light on him and
he danced. We did a class act."[5]

In the first year, "Rudolph" sold two and a half million copies.

Autry adds a postscript to the story, of how he later learned that Jonny Marks had sent "Rudolph" to Bing Crosby, Dinah Shore, and a number of other popular singers. "He added my name to the list as an afterthought."[6] "Rudolph" also seemed to have built a bond between Autry and Marks: "Every Christmas since 1949, Johnny calls. We chat about the latest sales figures for 'Rudolph,' and he wishes Ina and me the best of holiday greetings. He talks about 'Rudolph' as though he were real, and to Johnny he is, as our creations often tend to be. Somewhere in my home is a platinum record, which stands for the five-millionth copy sold. Not many singers ever get one of those. Old 'Rudolph' is pretty real to me, too."[7] Indeed, "Rudolph" changed Autry's direction as a performer, moving him from the country to the pop charts and revitalizing his career in the process.

On the face of Autry's story, it may be difficult to understand why he might pause at recording a catchy song like "Rudolph," especially when considered against the backdrop of the successful "Here Comes Santa Claus." At the time, however, Autry was still primarily a country music performer, and "Here Comes Santa Claus" had been a "one off." While "Rudolph," in retrospect, follows in the path of "Here Comes Santa Claus," Autry may have hesitated at focusing less on his country music base and more consciously pursuing a children's audience. "Rudolph," then, may have been weighed for more than its chart potential.

As with Autry's memories of recording "Rudolph," there seems to have been a long delay between the hit song in 1949 and Johnny Marks's recollections of how it came about. It would take time for journalists to even show interest in the songwriter who penned "Rudolph the Red-Nosed Reindeer"; as one newspaper article noted, "Johnny Marks became an overnight hero to millions in 1949, though few knew his name. He's a hero today, still behind the scenes."[8] And perhaps it took time for Marks to warm up to the idea of relating his "Rudolph" story. It was only in the mid-1970s, around the same time that Autry penned his autobiography, when Marks seems to have offered a full version of the birth and eventual success of "Rudolph the Red-Nosed Reindeer." In an Associated Press article from the winter of 1976, he touched on many of the same points as Autry:

1. Autry's initial rejection of "Rudolph"
2. Autry's change of mind when his wife, Ina, liked the song
3. Offering the song to Dinah Shore and Bing Crosby
4. Autry performing the song at the Madison Square Garden rodeo concert

Marks also emphasized his ongoing relationship with Autry, and added other elements that were more focused on his role in writing and developing the song. Before "Rudolph," Marks was an obscure songwriter, struggling to make ends meet. He first attempted to pen a song about Rudolph in 1948. "I wrote it—easily one of the worst songs ever written. It was just terrible. . . . Now what happened is, a year later, I'm walking along the street, it's never happened before, I started to hum. Dum di da-dum di dum-dum. You see, what I'm doing is inverting the notes, instead of going down, I'm going up."[9]

Because he felt like he had a hit, Marks then invested $25,000 to form St. Nicholas Music, a hefty sum, no doubt, at the time. This guaranteed that he would fully own "Rudolph," as opposed to sharing half the royalty with a song publishing company.

Even after Autry agreed to record the song, however, there was still no assurance it would be issued as a single, much less become a hit. Autry preferred "If It Doesn't Snow on Christmas," a song penned by Gerald Marks (no relation to Johnny) and Milton Pascal. Marks, however, had Ina Autry on his side and requested that Autry at least put "Rudolph" on the B side of the release. After Autry's performance at the Madison Square Garden rodeo, however, "Rudolph" seemed to be on its way. When issued by Columbia Records in September, the song became widely popular, making Marks a wealthy man. "Songwriter Johnny Marks expects to make $85,000 on his hit, 'Rudolph the Red-Nosed Etc,'" Walter Winchell wrote in 1949. "When he first brought it to Broadway everybody snubbed it. It's a kiddy platter."[10] By 1980, *People* noted that "Rudolph" had made millions for Marks, providing him with "more than 75 percent of his $800,000 annual income."[11]

Ever since, these stories by Autry and Marks have cued journalists on how to write about "Rudolph." Both the detail and angle of each seasonal write-up have been shaped by these talking points. Like May's origin story, Marks and Autry's "Rudolph" struggled from obscurity to win popular acclaim and gather riches for its creators. For most journalists, it was a story line too good to pass up.

Rewriting "Rudolph"

These stories, however, like the origin stories centered on May and Rudolph, had a number of variations. It would take Marks and Autry twenty-five years to settle on a narrative, and at that point, both stories more or less agreed or shadowed one another. Autry's version in particular became the standard for Christmas encyclopedias and books that focused—in three- or four-page write-ups—on Christmas songs.

Marks in particular, however, was rarely consistent. Memory, of course, accounts for many small differences. Autry, for instance, seems to remember recording all four Christmas songs at once and, in one version, in New York City. Instead, the four tracks were cut at two different recording sessions in Los Angeles. These details, though, make little difference to the overall shape of the narrative. The important points—Marks's penning the song, his choice of Autry to record it, Autry's initial rejection, the studio waxing of "Rudolph" at the last minute, the introduction of "Rudolph" at the rodeo in NYC, and the massive popularity of the song—remain intact.

Other variations are more confusing, partly because they complicate the story's arc, but also because they call into question the basic details of the birth of "Rudolph" and its early journey in 1948–49.

The actual background for recording "Rudolph" was less straightforward. As part of the process, Marks paid five dollars to have a demo of "Rudolph" cut by Guy Mitchell, a singer who would become popular in the early to mid-1950s. Technically, Mitchell recorded the first version of "Rudolph." That would have been the "home" demo that Marks shopped around to different singers in 1949.

Most likely Marks, like any other songwriter with new material, would have attempted to circulate the demo as widely as possible. In earlier interviews, Marks expanded on his choice of singers for "Rudolph": "That year I thought I had 10 recordings all lined up. All of them fell through. Crosby liked the song but did nothing about it. Como wasn't sure the kids would go for it. Eddy Howard recorded it but Mercury held it up a year so as not to compete with 'Mule Train,' his big hit. All I had left was Autry."[12] While Marks would indicate that Autry was far from his first choice, a great deal of thought had been put into choosing Autry nonetheless. Others within the music business, in fact, would play a role in convincing Marks that Autry *was* the right choice for the song. When an executive suggested the cowboy singer, Marks responded: "Gene Autry? He sings songs like 'Tumblin' Tumbleweeds' and 'The Last Roundup.' No, he's not the right singer."[13] Here, it is the unnamed executive (perhaps Mitch Miller) who persuades Marks to take a chance on Autry. In an earlier newspaper piece, Marks offers a slightly different version of this story, with a "friend at Warner Bros." making the suggestion, leading Marks to ask, "Why Autry?" His friend answered: "Because he has tremendous pull in the small towns."[14] While far from Marks's first choice for "Rudolph," Autry remained a calculated one.

One of the most intriguing variations on the "Rudolph" story originated from a Marks interview in 1969. Here, he told a reporter how he first came across a copy of May's poem. McCandlish Phillips wrote, "It was around 1939 that he [Marks] saw the Rudolph brochure—he does not remember exactly where—and jotted the title of it into a little notebook he carries.... He carried it around with him for almost a decade and finally put a few notes to the title in 1948."[15] Versions of this

Johnny Marks, *Rudolph the Red-Nosed Reindeer*, Spanish sheet music, date unknown | Papers of Robert L. May, Rauner Special Collections Library, Dartmouth College; courtesy of Dartmouth College Library

story line had been told as early as 1950. When suggesting that he first gathered a pamphlet of *Rudolph* before World War II, Marks seems to be distancing himself from May, his brother-in-law. If Marks knew of *Rudolph* before he married Margaret May (1947), then it may have offered him distance—both artistically and legally (copyright)—from Robert May. In his own scenario, Marks seems to come to Rudolph by his own accord, and the fact that his brother-in-law just happened to write the book is a coincidence. The coincidence is so glaring, however, that the whole scenario seems both unlikely and disingenuous. Possibly, once Marks's legal ownership of the song and subsequent projects became secure, he was more comfortable focusing on his first attempt to write "Rudolph" in 1948.

One point that no one seems to remember the same way is how the "Rudolph" demo came to Autry. In Holly George-Warren's biography of Autry (*Public Cowboy No. 1*), she spoke with Juanita Cotner, the widow of Autry's music director, Carl Cotner. In this version, Marks sent the "Rudolph" demo to Carl Cotner, asking him to sell it to Autry; he also offered him a piece of the action (a cut of the royalties). Cotner then told Autry, "I think it's a good song for you."[16] Cotner wrote an arrangement for "Rudolph," and during the session Autry asked, "How 'bout that song that you're so crazy about?"[17] Juanita Cotner continued: "They threw it up on the stands, and did it in one take. . . . [Later] a publicity man put it out that it was Ina that talked Gene into it."[18]

The Hecky Krasnow Variation

Perhaps the most fantastic story to come to light is also the most detailed. In her book *Rudolph, Frosty, and Captain Kangaroo*, Judy Gail Krasnow recalls her father's life as a musical producer and director. With the growing children's market for records, Columbia brought Krasnow in to oversee the children's and educational records department. In this role, he would work closely with Autry on a number of recordings, including "Peter Cottontail" and "Frosty the Snowman." Krasnow's first job as the director of children's music for Colombia Records was to record Autry singing "Rudolph the Red-Nosed Reindeer." In Judy Krasnow's rendering of her father's story, some of the elements of the Autry-Marks story remain, while others are inverted:

1. Krasnow discovers "Rudolph."
2. Krasnow believes that Autry is the right singer for "Rudolph."
3. Autry hesitates before agreeing to record the song.
4. Ina Autry asks her husband to record the song.
5. Autry is late to the June 27 recording session; he is also, when he arrives, drunk.
6. With studio time running out, Autry quickly records "Rudolph."

The Krasnow narrative begins with an argument between him and Columbia vice president Goddard Lieberson over the worth of "Rudolph" for a new release. The argument between the two also helps frame Rudolph's precarious balancing act as he entered the open market during the mid-to-late 1940s.

Krasnow believed that the song was sure to catch the attention of the millions

Gene Autry, *Merry*
Christmas with Gene
Autry (Columbia
Records, 1950).
The album held four
45 rpm records.

of children who had received free *Rudolph* books from Ward's. It was catchy and tuneful, and he believed—in his gut—that the kids would feel the same way. Lieberson argued the flip side. Six million books had been *given* away, not bought, which failed to guarantee *any* fan base. And even if all six million children had loved *Rudolph*, that only meant that the market was saturated.

Lieberson brought forward one other point that could—potentially—be argued today: Rudolph was not part of a traditional Christmas. Most Americans preferred tradition when it came to holidays like Christmas, and attempting to market a new angle would only fall flat. Finally, Lieberson brought out a complaint left over from the 1930s: Christmas records could only be sold between Thanksgiving and Christmas, leaving a very small window for sales.

Despite Lieberson's misgivings, he allowed Krasnow to continue: he would succeed or fail on his own. Even with a green light, however, Krasnow's complications continued. He believed that Columbia recording artist Gene Autry had a "warmth and naturalness" that "would appeal to all ages,"[19] making him the right person to record "Rudolph." Lieberson argued with him on this point as well, saying, "Hecky, how could you even consider a cowboy? This is children's music, not country and western, not pop!"[20] Autry seemed to agree and took his time returning Krasnow's phone calls. Autry still expressed doubts about the song but told Krasnow he would record it because "Ina says I should do it."[21] They set the recording date for June 27 at 10 a.m.

On the day of the session, everything was in place in the studio except for one detail: by 10:30 a.m., Autry had still not arrived. The Carl Cotner Orchestra and Pinafores warmed up, practicing "Rudolph" as another half hour went by. Finally, Autry arrived with his wife Ina, but Krasnow quickly noticed that there was a problem. "He didn't have to be told that Gene had imbibed too much Christmas cheer well before the holiday season."[22] Initially, Autry was in no shape to record, but Ina ordered milk and orange juice, and soon the cowboy singer had returned to form, with twenty minutes left in the session. After a quick adjustment to the recording dials and a brief interruption in the form of a phone call from Lieberson, everything fell into place and "Rudolph" was recorded in one full take.

In this version, the choice of song and singer, and even the last-minute recording of "Rudolph," were primarily accomplished by Krasnow's vision and efforts. And clearly this story, like the variations by Marks, clashes with the "Rudolph" origin story most commonly told today.

The Real "Rudolph"?

Once a song like "Rudolph" becomes a massive hit, everyone wishes to know its origin. No one, it seems, cares how "If It Doesn't Snow on Christmas" was recorded. As with May's creation of *Rudolph*, these stories often seem more like myths-as-works-in-progress than the result of memory. The story evolves and keeps getting better; as time passes, the people who tell these stories become more central to the narrative.

Gene Autry, "Rudolph the Red-Nosed Reindeer" (Columbia Records, 1950)

Marks's variations are perhaps the most problematic. He consistently claimed that he never meant to write a Christmas song and that even "Rudolph" was never intended as one. "The funny thing is," Marks told a newspaper writer, "that it was only by accident that the song had a Christmas theme. Anybody who sits down and says he'll write a Christmas song is welcome to try—but I'll guarantee it won't be a good one."[23] It is difficult to believe, however, that Marks never viewed "Rudolph" as a Christmas song.

Complicating Marks's contribution to the Rudolph narrative is that there is a lack of information—a cache of letters, a remembrance by a friend, or an off-the-cuff interview—that provides a good feel for the person who wrote the song. In some interviews Marks comes across as indifferent toward "Rudolph," as though he had become bored with Christmas and his famous song. Regarding the money he made from royalties on "Rudolph," Marks told *Time* in 1960, "What the hell, I can't control the American way of life. I'm not going to fight it; I'm going to join it." And, "If I sell that many at Christmastime, what the hell do I care what they do in May?"[24] Marks seemingly lacked the warmth and optimism exuded by May and is described in one newspaper piece as appearing like a Wall Street broker. Occasionally, this makes "Rudolph" seem more of a business venture than a song for kids. In regard to the "Rudolph" origin story, it becomes difficult to gain an accurate view of Marks's various versions.

In a radio interview from 1976 Marks offered a different version of how he came to Rudolph. The interview, however, only appeared in book form in 2012. Again, in earlier interviews, Marks had suggested he found the story of *Rudolph* before the war and filed it away; this presumably would have been the booklet distributed by Montgomery Ward in 1939. In the 1976 radio interview, however, Marks seems less guarded. Here, he also explains more fully how he wrote "Rudolph":

> I've been asked, I don't know how many times, how the song came about. My brother-in-law, Robert May, happened to send me a little book about this character called Rudolph. . . . Well, you know the story. . . . By 1947, there were some six million copies given away or sold and it was a year later that I got hold of a copy. I was working with Carmen Lombardo at the time and felt so strongly that Robert May's story was an ideal subject on which to base a song. . . . I finally got something that I thought was decent and I took it to Carmen to ask his opinion. He said, "Johnny, that's a great song. In fact, my brother [Guy Lombardo] might even do it."[25]

This seems a likely account of the process. Sending the book, May likely commissioned, gave permission, or simply implied that Marks should write a song about Rudolph.

The Krasnow narrative poses other problems while also filling in previously unavailable details. It would be easy to be critical of Judy Gail Krasnow's narrative of her father's life; it is both secondhand and too far removed from the original events. These are fair points, but the issue of distance can be brought to bear on most of Marks's and Autry's stories about "Rudolph": only later, after mass fame, does each of their stories appear in full form.

The Krasnow narrative does fill in a missing part of Autry's story: for several years, Krasnow produced Autry's recordings, including "Frosty the Snowman" and "Peter Cottontail." Autry never mentions this in *Back in the Saddle Again*, and there seems an attempt—in the Autry camp—to write Krasnow out of the picture. When asked in an interview whether Carl Cotner produced the "Rudolph" session, Autry associate Alex Gordon answered: "Yes. He was in charge of that session. He did the arrangement and conducted the orchestra. He produced the recording but didn't pick the song."[26]

Autry does seem to allude to Krasnow or another Columbia manager in *Back in the Saddle Again* when he notes that the session did not go smoothly: "There was an argument with the A&R man over a point that no longer matters, if it did at the time, and everything seemed to drag. The job of the A&R man—the initials stand for artist and repertoire—is to look for songs and artists and fit the two together. In those days he also acted as the producer—if you let him."[27] Others were more specific about the clash between Krasnow and Autry. Don Cusic, in his *Gene Autry: His Life and Career*, wrote: "Johnny Bond remembered that Autry and his new producer were not getting along well during the recording of the Christmas songs. Bond recalled they spent a great deal of time recording the selections. 'We thought they would never get the takes to his satisfaction, but they did.'"[28]

Whatever the realities of the relationship between Autry and his producer, Krasnow's position at Columbia would have provided him with the leverage needed to make key choices. Krasnow, then, was involved in the "Rudolph" session and a player in the attention "Rudolph" received from Columbia.

Weighing the available information, "Rudolph" seems to have been written by Marks after receiving a copy of *Rudolph the Red-Nosed Reindeer* from his brother-in-law Robert May in 1948–49. Marks's authorship helped establish a second "Rudolph" copyright, perhaps creating an intersecting or dual ownership of the franchise. After rewriting "Rudolph" in the spring of 1949, Marks paid Guy Mitchell five dollars to record a "Rudolph" demo. That demo was circulated to at least ten singers, including Perry Como, Bing Crosby, Eddy Howard, and

Gene Autry. Eventually, all these prospects fell through, save for Autry. Initially, however, even Autry was reluctant to record "Rudolph," partly, perhaps, because of fears of being pigeonholed as a children's singer.

In time, however, Autry was persuaded or pressured to record "Rudolph" in a Los Angles studio in the summer of 1949. The "Rudolph" session was the inaugural session for producer Hecky Krasnow, hired by Columbia to oversee its children's records department. At this session and perhaps over time, Krasnow and Autry had a difficult relationship. After studio adjustments and perhaps a false start, "Rudolph" seems to have been recorded in one take. With the song now "in the can," "Rudolph" proved a crowd pleaser for Autry in September at the annual rodeo at Madison Square Garden.

At this point, the story seems to come to a dead end. "Rudolph," the familiar story suggests, was a natural, which guaranteed that millions of singles would be sold. But as with May and Ward's preparation of the *Rudolph* book, recording "Rudolph" was only the first step toward fame and fortune. Now it would be Marks, Autry, and Columbia's job to prep the ground for the forthcoming "Rudolph" single. To guarantee that every American child would get onboard the "Rudolph" juggernaut, a massive campaign—with concert performances, artwork, ads, and radio promotion—would have to be put in motion. As summer turned into fall, this is exactly what happened.

six

SELLING "RUDOLPH"

It would take at least six months to prepare "Rudolph the Red-Nosed Reindeer" for its public reception in the fall and winter of 1949. Johnny Marks wrote "Rudolph" in the spring, Autry recorded it during the summer, and Columbia Records most likely spent the remaining part of the summer and early fall on artwork and promotion. In retrospect, "Rudolph" seemed like a natural. Marks, after all, *knew* he would have a hit, just as Ina Autry believed in the reindeer underdog, and producer Hecky Krasnow had a gut instinct. In real time, however, a tremendous effort was being put into making "Rudolph" a success, and even then, no one could be sure.

"Rudolph" followed in the footsteps of Autry's "Here Comes Santa Claus" from 1947, a novelty holiday song geared toward the quickly growing children's market for records. While the novelty song itself had a long history, the children's Christmas song—like the modern Christmas song itself ("White Christmas," "The Christmas Song")—was no more than a few years old. As the baby boom surged forward in 1946, songs like Spike Jones's "All I Want for Christmas Is My Two Front Teeth" looked at the holiday from a child's point of view. When Autry's "Here Comes Santa Claus" returned to the charts in 1948, and when other performers like Bing Crosby also recorded the song, it was easy to see the logic for Autry and others to record new holiday material specifically for children.

The novelty Christmas song itself, however, was subsumed under the larger banner of children's records, a genre that began growing tremendously after World War II. And the word "tremendously" should not be underestimated here. *Billboard* surveyed the change: "The kidisk Christmas biz boom is on. Waxeries are flooding department stores and record shops thruout the country with more moppet material than ever before. Survey of area's [Hollywood] department stores reveals the estimated kiddie album sale reaching 20 to 25 per cent of total pre-Yuletide record biz, with some saying this is indicative of the national trend."[1] These recordings included pop and novelty songs (Fred Waring's "'Twas the Night before Christmas"), classics suitable for children (Ronald Colman's version of *A Christmas Carol*), and other spoken-word records like Paul Wing's RCA outing of *Rudolph the Red-Nosed Reindeer* in 1947. *Billboard* began tracking children's recordings—both musical and spoken word—in 1948. And while the market for children's records would be undermined by a number of changes in the mid-1950s (including television and rock and roll), this "golden age" of kid disks would have an incredible run.

As the era kicked off, one challenge for record labels was how a particular performer might fit into this new genre. Performers, too, were wary of being relegated to preteens. Autry, for instance, was a country and western singer who also starred in western movies; Bing Crosby was a crooner and movie star, an idol and a leading man. When labels pushed these performers in new directions, many established singers must have paused: why, after years of cultivating an audience, change course now? But the youth audience promised a new base of record buyers. With children and Christmas already the perfect match, the addition of children's records for Christmas seemed a natural extension.

Even without this new trend, Christmas proved the best time of year for *all* record sales. And while "Rudolph" and other holiday singles would have only two months to hit the charts and appear in stores, they had a potential advantage. If a single like "Rudolph" by an artist like Autry caught on, the single could return to the charts for several years. Christmas may have come only once a year, but it came *every* year.

Groundwork

Today there is a constant stream of commentary from mid-October to early November over one simple question: how early is too early for Christmas songs? Should the retail season, with holiday tunes serving as an aural backdrop, begin the day after Halloween or wait until after the Thanksgiving weekend?

In truth, however, the debate is quite old, and the seasonal timetable guarantees that a great deal of groundwork would precede the purchase of "Rudolph" or any holiday record or product. Autry prepared the way by performing the song as early as October. On October 8, Autry broadcast a version of "Rudolph" for his *Melody Ranch* radio program on CBS, live from New York City. Johnny Bond, a musician who worked with Autry, kicks off the performance asking, "Say, who's Rudolph?" "Well, Johnny," Autry replies, "'Rudolph the Red-Nosed Reindeer' is a song that I recorded just a while back, and well even though it may seem like we're rushing the season just a little, I think you'll agree that the story of Rudolph is worth it. So why don't you just listen while I tell the folks all about him, huh?"[2]

Johnny Marks, apparently, asked Autry to sing "Rudolph" at one or more of his rodeo performances at Madison Square Garden, going so far as to purchase a Rudolph suit. As Autry sang "Rudolph," band member Frankie Marvin donned the suit and danced in a blue spotlight.

Later, Autry would worry less about "rushing the season": fans wanted to hear "Rudolph" whatever the time of year. On the air and in concert, Autry would do his part to promote the new Columbia single.

The Madison Square Garden rodeo was a big event in New York City and garnered coverage by the Associated Press and *Billboard*. "Broadway looks like a cow trail today as scores of cowboys, cowgirls and Indian braves stroll in the wake of Gene Autry for the 24th annual world's championship rodeo at Madison Square Garden."[3] Mail-order tickets went on sale the week of August 27, and the rodeo opened on September 28. Autry, the singing cowboy, drew on a broad fan base and the backing of the gigantic Columbia records. "Gene Autry and his horse, Champion," wrote *Billboard*, "will be the feature attraction once more."[4]

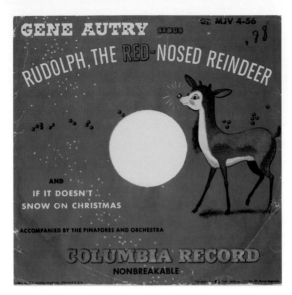

Gene Autry, "Rudolph the Red-Nosed Reindeer," 45 rpm recording (Columbia Records, 1951)

Autry received more coverage in *Billboard* on October 8 under the headline "Autry Gets in Plugs for His Columbia Wax." Autry, the magazine noted, "did his usual creditable selling job with *Riders in the Sky*, which is also the title of his new flicker which Columbia Pictures will release shortly."[5] Other activities flourished around the rodeo, including a performance aboard a special train junket for Connecticut rodeo patrons.

Autry's version of "Rudolph the Red-Nosed Reindeer" was issued the week of September 17, 1949. *Billboard* (using a variant spelling for Krasnow) ran a notice:

AUTRY'S DISKS FOR KIDS

New York, Sept. 17—Columbia Records will release Gene Autry's waxing of *Rudolph, the Red-Nosed Reindeer* and *If It Doesn't Snow at Christmas* as a children's record this week, but has no plans to issue the platter in the pop field in the immediate future, according to Hecky Krasno, the label's kidisk topper. Despite the pop nature of the coupling it will be pressed on vinylite and issued in a special kidisk package, to retail at $1.19.[6]

While it may have seemed early for Christmas records, Columbia obviously wanted to have everything primed—records pressed and shipped, along with notices and advertisements in *Billboard*—when the season arrived.

Appearing two weeks later in the October 1 issue of *Billboard*, an advertisement seemingly paid for by St. Nicholas Music announced the arrival of "Rudolph": "For this year and every year, the fabulous novelty song, 'Rudolph the Red-Nosed Reindeer.'"[7] Interestingly, the ad mentions Gene Autry *and* Eddy Howard as the two singers who had recorded the song; but as mentioned earlier, Howard's Mercury Records version was held back until the following year. In a special issue of *Billboard*, "Rudolph" was listed as one of the "songs with greatest radio audiences."[8] In the regular issue of *Billboard* from October 22, a headline read, "Columbia Preps Large Issue of Christmas Matter on L P." "In the past," the article noted, "Columbia has pioneered several outstanding singles in the Christmas line, such as *Here Comes Santa Claus*. . . . The diskery's Christmas line-up also includes new Autry material, including *He's a Chubby Little Fellow* and *Santa, Santa, Santa*. The highly publicized *Rudolph the Red Nosed Reindeer* has also been cut by Autry for Columbia."[9]

The enormous push for "Rudolph" by Marks, Columbia, and Autry makes several things clear. First, if Autry had initially been reluctant to record "Rudolph," he fell in line with Columbia's fall promotion for the single. Next, while articles and interviewees frequently mention that "Rudolph" began as a B side (Marks repeated this story), the promotion push surely singled "Rudolph" out as the A side. And finally, when articles about Autry and "Rudolph" along with advertising by Marks and Columbia ran in *Billboard*, this guaranteed that the industry (disk jockeys, radio station managers, distributors, and department and record stores) would be fully aware of the imminent release. Everything that could be done to prepare a new single for the biggest and most receptive audience had been done for "Rudolph."

Billboard Charts

One thing that would help Autry's "Rudolph" a great deal in 1949 must have seemed, initially, like a drawback to Marks: it was the *only* recording of "Rudolph." While this fact may seem unremarkable today, it was quite common for record labels to quickly latch onto a new hit by a rival label, rushing a performer from its roster into the studio to produce a competing disk. A guess as to why this failed to happen with "Rudolph" would point to the extremely short season for promoting a holiday record: by the time a new disk could be recorded, manufactured, and made available at the local Sears, Roebuck, Christmas buying would have been over. One recording of "Rudolph" meant that all the radio play and purchases of the song were concentrated on Columbia/Autry's version, which meant that no other "Rudolph" singles were diluting chart positions and sales.

After what must have seemed like several very long weeks to Marks and Autry, "Rudolph" appeared on *Billboard*'s children's records chart for the first time on November 12, 1949. The song rested at number eleven, sandwiched between "Little Orley–Uncle Lumpy" and "Bugs Bunny and the Tortoise."[10] Early in September when Krasnow spoke with *Billboard*, this positioning on the children's chart was exactly what had been expected. There were other good signs in the same *Billboard* issue. "Rudolph" was listed as second, behind Ernest Tubb's "Blue Christmas," as a possible top-played record by disk jockeys. "Rudolph" was also slotted for a special promotion program by Columbia and appeared once again on "The Top 30 Tunes" with the greatest potential for radio audiences. Finally, *Billboard* seemed to foresee a promising future for the song. "With Gene Autry's cutting of *Rudolph the Red-Nose Reindeer* shaping up as the diskery's biggest all-time children's hit, Krasno heads for the Coast in a couple weeks to cut more material by the Western star."[11]

"Rudolph" continued to move up the charts, jumping to number six on November 19, tying for first with "Bozo and the Birds" on November 26, and standing alone at number one on December 3. Another curious thing, however, was happening: "Rudolph" had spilled over from the children's chart and was now making a showing on the pop charts. By December 10 it had become vividly clear that something special was happening with "Rudolph." Under a subheading of "Reindeer Hot," *Billboard* wrote: "Most talked about of the new seasonal items is Columbia's etching of Rudolph the Red Nosed Reindeer. The waxing, which was issued originally as a kidisk, was released later on both pop and folk listings following an early immediate demand for the record. The record . . . this week achieved a peak in sale Tuesday (29), when it sold 102,000 platters in the one day. The platter will have done about 600,000 at the end of this week."[12]

Interestingly, as "Rudolph" continued to move up and down the children's chart, it was joined by Paul Wing's narrative version of the book, *Rudolph the Red-Nosed Reindeer*, from 1947. On the week of December 10, the song was at seven and the book at six.

Even with this success, it was only in mid-December when Columbia prepared its biggest promotion for "Rudolph." With a solid recording and heavy promotion, "Rudolph" remained on the children's records chart for fifteen weeks, spilling over into 1950.

"Rudolph the Red-Nosed Reindeer," 1950

To say that "Rudolph" was popular or even very popular is to misname the song's cultural impact. There were many other popular songs in 1949, including Christmas songs, but most of these songs are forgotten today. "Rudolph," however, was a phenomenon. While the success of "Rudolph" created a sensation in 1949, his long-term place as Santa's lead reindeer would become evident only during the 1950 holiday season. On October 14 of that year, *Billboard* noted, "Columbia's major push is based on its fabulously successful Gene Autry waxings. Autry, whose rodeo is now playing to about 200,000 people weekly, still features his *Rudolph, the Red-Nosed Reindeer* routine, and is adding a new one on *Frosty, the Snowman*. Columbia distribs have been asked to carry the ball on local Autry tie-ins and department store displays for both *Rudolph* and *Frosty* characters. . . . The diskery itself is providing a new array of point-of-sale material for all kid albums."[13] While Columbia obviously hoped that "Frosty," Autry's new Christmas disk in 1950, would repeat the success of "Rudolph," the "Rudolph" single continued to get a great deal of attention from the label.

Robert May, *Rudolph the Red-Nosed Reindeer*, the Paul Wing spoken version, on two 78 rpm records (RCA, 1947) | Papers of Robert L. May, Rauner Special Collections Library, Dartmouth College; courtesy of Dartmouth College Library

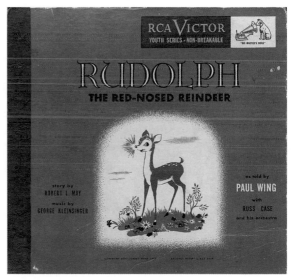

Marks published an ad in *Billboard* at the beginning of November 1950, listing the sixteen performers (including Autry) who had recorded the song. Sheet music sales, once the main indicator of a song's success, remained strong. "*Rudolph the Red-Nosed Reindeer*, last year's runaway Christmas leader, is off to a merry gallop . . . having sold over 110,000 copies of sheet music since August for writer-publisher Johnny Marks."[14] And Autry's recording itself, a year old, was selling briskly in the early fall. "The Gene Autry disking on Columbia sold 232,933 . . . [in] July, August and September. Since the waxery didn't really open up on the tune till after Labor Day, it's a fair guess most of the sales came in September. It's the leading current pop seller at Columbia now by a good margin."[15] Columbia also made sure that the recording would be available in a number of formats: as a pop 78 rpm, a children's 78 rpm, as a seven-inch pop LP, a seven-inch children's LP, and as a 45 rpm recording. Later in 1950, a ten-inch LP would be issued. Of the LP, *Billboard* wrote: "With three definite hits included, and with the magic of Autry's name, this one should find its way into thousands of stockings Christmas Eve. Santa Claus and the nation's disk dealers reportedly are ordering heavy."[16] "Meanwhile," a *Billboard* writer noted, "arrangements have been made for a *Rudolph* float in Macy's Thanksgiving Day parade."[17]

It helped considerably that Autry remained very popular, even outside of "Rudolph" and other holiday songs like "Peter Cottontail" and "Frosty the Snowman." In November 1950, Krasnow put together *Gene Autry at the Rodeo*, a $3.40 two-record set, complete with a picture book. Columbia added its weight in the November 18 issue of *Billboard*, taking out an entire page with a head shot of Autry and featuring two Johnny Marks releases, "Rudolph" and "When Santa Claus Gets Your Letter."

In 1950 "Rudolph" behaved more like a new single than a year-old disk and continued to receive support from Marks, Autry, and Columbia. Combined with the continuing efforts of Montgomery Ward and Robert May, "Rudolph" the fad now seemed like an ongoing trend. In records sold (another million in 1950), versions recorded (at least sixteen), and pop cultural recognition, the red-nosed reindeer was outpacing all the competition.

The Golden Age of Children's Records

The second factor that helped push "Rudolph" into the stratosphere of success centered on the vital market for children's records after World War II. Peter Muldavin has labeled the years between 1946 and 1956 as the golden age of kiddie records and offers five items that kicked off the craze:

1. The replacement of brittle shellac disks by durable vinyl
2. The production of colorful record sleeves and colorful vinyl records
3. The availability of inexpensive record players
4. The availability of inexpensive records
5. The competitive market that created a high-quality product[18]

The market, then, was perfectly situated for the arrival of the boom.

As with picture books like *Rudolph*, the baby boom promised what seemed like an endless expansion for kid disks during the 1940s and 1950s. Still, the initial success of children's records like "Rudolph" seemed to catch record labels and performers by surprise. One day no label or artist considered it important to cater to children; the next, labels and artists were tripping over themselves to meet demand. "Sales of children's records have skyrocketed in the short space of four years, from seven million in 1944 to fifty million in 1947," noted Philip Eisenberg and Hecky Krasnow. There were, the writers continued, "600 different titles on the market, six times as many as 1944."[19]

Within the music business in the latter half of the 1940s, the children's market would become one of the most important revenue sources for labels. Eisenberg and Krasnow stated that children's records accounted for "approximately fifteen per cent of the entire record business."[20] By the early 1950s, children's disks equaled 25 percent of the industry's sales and roughly half of holiday sales.

Initially, however, none of this was clear. Many worried in 1946 that too much faith was being placed in the "kidisk boom." "Many stores are becoming so heavily stocked with the moppet packages that unless their Christmas business on the albums reaches record-breaking figures, there will be plenty of returns to the distribs when the holidays are over."[21] Two months later, however, a *Billboard* headline read, "Dark Pre-Yule Picture Fails to Jell as Kidisk Sales Soar."[22] Still, few could believe that such massive sales could be repeated. "Feeling among some retailers is that they will never again see the 1946 Christmas peak."[23] The kidisk market, however, was just warming up.

In *Spoken Word: Postwar American Phonograph Cultures*, Jacob Smith expands on the reasons for this golden era, noting the many places that children found records during the latter half of the 1940s and throughout the 1950s. While the primary listening space was the home, records for children were everywhere. Libraries, for instance, began carrying recordings and, over time, began lending these just like other materials. Schools also used recordings to supplement teaching methods. With the expansion of peewee platters, the traditional record shop became more child friendly, while department stores made room for the new merchandise. And although parents continued to purchase many of these recordings for children, increasingly children shopped for their own records. "This year [1947] more than ever," Thomas Sugrue wrote in the *Saturday Review*, "the record shop is a friendly environment for the child shopper."[24]

The colorful sleeves themselves, a component of the golden era, made the advertising pitch directly to children. On both 78 rpm and 45 rpm Columbia singles, Rudolph is the prominent image on the sleeve. On the 78 in particular, Rudolph stands front and center against a blue background. Rudolph's image is likewise featured on the Paul Wing recordings of *Rudolph the Red-Nosed Reindeer* in 1947 and *Rudolph's Second Christmas* in 1951, both for RCA. In the 1947 RCA album (containing two 78 rpm records), scenes similar to those from the book have been reproduced, maintaining a continuity with the published *Rudolph*. Columbia reserved the back of the 45 rpm release to suggest other titles, like "The Little Engine That Could" and "Frosty the Snowman." In both cases, RCA and Columbia worked hard to create images that would gain the young listener's attention, leading to either a request for a parent to buy the disk, or the child using his or her own money to buy the record.

The very newness of the market in the latter half of the 1940s also highlighted

Robert May, *Rudolph's Second Christmas*, 45 rpm record (RCA, 1951)

Robert May, *Rudolph's Second Christmas*, record jacket (RCA, 1951). The set included two 45 rpm records.

a number of unknowns: no one was sure how to take advantage of it. No one could be certain, for instance, that an artist like Gene Autry would even sell to children, or whether his older country and western fans would be put off by this new emphasis. Did those who loved "Riders in the Sky" also want to hear Autry sing "Rudolph the Red-Nosed Reindeer"? No one could be certain. Columbia, one reviewer noted, "apparently believes in trying everything." "It includes," the reviewer continued, "the 'pop' song variety, which reached its height with 'Rudolph the Red-Nosed Reindeer.'"[25] "Rudolph" would change Autry's career, edging him toward the children's market and pop charts. Columbia, raking in the profits from "Rudolph," quickly lined up new seasonal favorites like "Peter Cottontail" and "Frosty the Snowman" for Autry.

Rudolph . . . 1950, 1951, and 1952

Dozens and finally hundreds of versions of "Rudolph" would proliferate on record labels big and small, but the song's initial success on the charts would be bolstered by performers who sang for Decca (Bing Crosby and Red Foley) and RCA Victor (Spike Jones). These companies, along with Columbia, housed many of the most popular performers of the era, allowing generous promotion budgets, distribution at record and discount stores, and a sympathetic fan base for the latest single by their artists. With big-league support, "Rudolph" easily spilled over into the early 1950s.

One repeated "Rudolph" story is that Bing Crosby turned down the chance to record the song in 1949. Autry told disk jockey Casey Kasem how Crosby, on a break during a recording session, asked him to shake hands with the man who had turned down "Rudolph." The truth of the story is less intriguing than what it implies: that "Rudolph," the underdog, persevered despite the initial rejection by a major recording star. Furthermore, the story suggests that "Rudolph" was at least considered by a very important performer of the time. What gets lost in the telling, however, is that Crosby *did* record "Rudolph" the following year and that his hit—while perhaps less stellar than Autry's—was nonetheless one of the biggest of the 1950 holiday season.

As the most popular Christmas crooner of his time, Crosby, along with his record label, would have been anxious to have a single ready for the fall of 1950. Like Autry, however, Crosby may have had reservations about singing for children. Whatever his misgivings, and whether or not these played a role in his initial rejection of "Rudolph," he quickly changed his mind. For the B side, Decca slated another children's favorite, "Teddy Bear's Picnic."

Red Foley also recorded "Rudolph" in 1950, though it would have to wait until 1951 to become a hit. In fact, "Rudolph" was only the B side, with "Frosty the Snowman" serving as the lead track. Both, however, were big hits and would share chart and radio space with both the Autry and Crosby versions of "Rudolph."

At this point, everyone involved—record labels, recording artists, and *Billboard*—must have been amazed at the song's extended shelf life. In the day-to-day workings of the music business, one popular recording quickly faded to make room for a new one. "Rudolph," however, just kept giving, returning to the charts each year as Santa Claus's permanent sidekick.

Bing Crosby, "Rudolph the Red-Nosed Reindeer," 45 rpm recording (Decca, circa 1950)

Rudolph the Red-Nosed Reindeer Picture Book, 1951 | Papers of Robert L. May, Rauner Special Collections Library, Dartmouth College; courtesy of Dartmouth College Library

seven

THE BRAND-NEW ADVENTURES OF RUDOLPH THE RED-NOSED REINDEER

Following Autry's "Rudolph the Red-Nosed Reindeer" in 1949, the young reindeer's fame knew no bounds. As the 1950s dawned, Rudolph had gone from the recognizable reindeer at the local Ward's store to a national pop idol. Until the fall of 1949, it would have been quite possible for an older couple with no young children at home to have never heard of Santa Claus's new sidekick. Likewise, most European children remained perfectly happy with the eight traditional reindeer from "A Visit from St. Nicholas." Now Rudolph had moved to the A-list, rubbing shoulders with Mickey Mouse, Bugs Bunny, and Woody Woodpecker.

Rudolph's newfound prestige simultaneously boosted previous efforts by May and created a number of new opportunities. In the wake of these opportunities, May left Ward's for seven years during the 1950s, managing the activities of his red-nosed protégé full time. It is often noted in articles about May and Rudolph that his family grew rich from the proceeds of Rudolph the Red-Nosed Reindeer Enterprises. May, and later May's children, attempted to correct this view. The truth, they contended, was much more modest. Rudolph helped buy a new home for the May family, sent the children to college, and allowed for the rare luxury of foreign travel. Still, for a few years Rudolph required May's services full time.

During this time, the Mays initiated their own folk tradition involving Rudolph. Each Christmas, "they'll place a lighted life sized figure of Rudolph on

the lawn and think for awhile of their reindeer's ride to fame and fortune."[1] This eight-foot reindeer made it easy to find May and his family. "Neighborhood children know him as the man 'who made Rudolph.'"[2]

May was initially reluctant to allow any Rudolph sequels, either in book or song form. During the 1950s, however, he wrote two new Rudolph stories, one that was released as a spoken-word record by RCA in 1951 and another that became his second Rudolph print book for Maxton in 1954. Little Golden Books, established by Simon & Schuster in 1942, would also print a prose version of *Rudolph the Red-Nosed Reindeer* adapted by Barbara Shook Hazen in 1958. During this same period a serialized Rudolph appeared in seasonal newspaper comics and an annual DC comic book. Choosing from a smorgasbord of printed materials, kids could read about Rudolph's new adventures, color his nose red, and even see him materialize in 3-D form from a pop-up book.

Like Coca-Cola and Santa Claus, Rudolph would be exported to England, Australia, the Netherlands, and many other countries. "That reindeer is becoming a Canadian tradition," Quebec's *St. Maurice Valley Chronicle* wrote in 1960. "From a small beginning in 1938, the little animal with the built-in beacon has become as familiar as Humpty-Dumpty and Cinderella to youngsters everywhere."[3]

The proliferation of story lines, however, created certain challenges. All Rudolph stories—comic strips, comic books, and children's books—faced similar limitations. Each Rudolph story line would be hemmed in by his likable personality, his place within the Santa Claus myth, and the Christmas season. Like other cartoon and comic book characters, he never seemed to age, and if he did change—as when he becomes self-pitying in *Rudolph Shines Again*—everything

Robert L. May and Rube Grossman, *Rensdyret Rudolf med den røde tud* (Danish adaptation of *Rudolph the Red-Nosed Reindeer*), circa 1950s | Papers of Robert L. May, Rauner Special Collections Library, Dartmouth College; courtesy of Dartmouth College Library

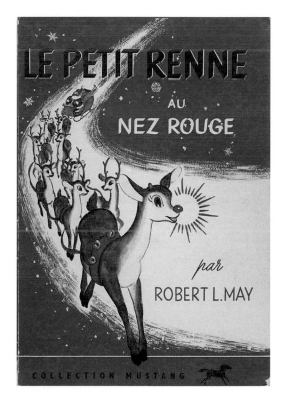

Robert L. May, *Le petit renne au nez rouge* (French translation of *Rudolph the Red-Nosed Reindeer*), 1952 | Papers of Robert L. May, Rauner Special Collections Library, Dartmouth College; courtesy of Dartmouth College Library

reverts by the end of the story. The Rudolph set-up, then, might be described as a North Pole sitcom.

Because of Rudolph's age, the stories generally remained geared for the youngest readers. This was another reason why he could never grow up. While comic books would require more reading skills than *Rudolph's Second Christmas*, they still relied heavily on visuals and were designed for the youngest readers (preteens, six to twelve). This meant that even when crises or villains appeared, they were never overly threatening. Rudolph, at the end of the day, still had to be the innocent child hero who saves—once again—Christmas.

May's Sequels and Little Golden Books' *Rudolph the Red-Nosed Reindeer*

In 1951 May wrote a second Rudolph story, *Rudolph's Second Christmas*, issued as a spoken-word recording. Like *Rudolph*'s previous spoken-word record, it would be narrated by Paul Wing and released on RCA. Until much later (1992), *Rudolph's Second Christmas* remained unpublished in book form.

When Rudolph discovers a letter from Sonny and Sis, two children Santa Claus has missed on Christmas Eve, he embarks on a journey to find them. The children's parents operate a traveling circus, and since the circus is unpopular, they move frequently. When Rudolph finally finds the circus, he understands why it is so unpopular: there is a toothless tiger and a mouse shot out of a pop-gun, among other oddities. On his way back home, Rudolph meets a number of strange creatures in the forest: a dog that meows and a cat that barks; a canary that talks and a parrot that never learned to say "Polly want a cracker."[4] When these animals—at Rudolph's suggestion—join the Silly Circus, it becomes a big hit.

Perhaps the most intriguing aspect of *Rudolph's Second Christmas*, as author Tim Hollis has noted, is the similarity between the forest animals and the characters on the Island of Misfit Toys in Rankin/Bass's *Rudolph* special from 1964 (more on this in chapter 9). Like Rudolph himself, May seems to root for all the misfits of the world.

Rudolph the Red-Nosed Reindeer Shines Again was published by Maxton in 1954. Once again, Rudolph is ostracized by the other reindeer, though this time he is singled out for being famous. Rudolph reacts by feeling sorry for himself, eventually causing the light in his nose to fade. Fearing he is no longer of use to Santa Claus, he runs away into the forest. There he meets a pair of rabbit parents whose children, Donnie and Doris, have been lost in the woods. Rudolph is determined to find them, even though his nose is of no help. Eventually, with the help of an angel, he locates the lost bunnies and—running from a wolf—returns them safely home. Thanks to his unselfish act, Rudolph's nose begins to work again.

Perhaps the most unexpected element in *Rudolph Shines Again* is the appearance of an angel, a figure of religious significance in a story line (Rudolph's) that had been primarily secular. Arguably, the appearance of the angel seems out of place.

Robert L. May, *Rudolph the Red-Nosed Reindeer Shines Again*, illustrated by Marion Guild, 1954 | Papers of Robert L. May, Rauner Special Collections Library, Dartmouth College; courtesy of Dartmouth College Library

While millions of copies of the original *Rudolph* had been given away and sold by the mid-1950s, there was nonetheless one element of the book that seemed old-fashioned: May's poetic meter. Even as early as 1940, a publishing editor who had expressed interest in May's writing noted that there was little market for poetry. When the Maxton edition of *Rudolph* came out in 1947, new illustrations accompanied May's poem. When the Little Golden Books edition came out in 1958, it would have new illustrations *and* be written as prose. Furthermore, a new writer would be brought in, Barbara Shook Hazen, to adapt the story. In essence, Little Golden Books brought *Rudolph* into line with the other children's books of the day, basically replacing the earlier editions. For many baby boomers, Hazen's prose and Richard Scarry's images of Rudolph remain the most familiar.

Robert L. May,
*Rudolph the Red-Nosed
Reindeer*, adapted by
Barbara Shook Hazen
and illustrated by
Richard Scarry, 1958
| Papers of Robert
L. May, Rauner
Special Collections
Library, Dartmouth
College; courtesy of
Dartmouth College
Library

While the "adapted" *Rudolph* retains many elements of the original, the story varies in several significant ways. Rudolph still has a shiny red nose, and the other reindeer still make fun of him. Unlike the original, however, in which he lived in a small village with his mother and father, Rudolph now lives in Toyland. The main addition to the story line is "Santa's Team-Choosing Time," the contest that will help pick out the strongest, fastest, and most surefooted reindeer for Christmas Eve. Because Rudolph is afraid that Santa will dislike his nose, he hides in a chest built by the elves and, as a result of his absence, becomes the only reindeer who does not receive an assigned task to complete. He finally decides to face the ridicule of the other reindeer because he wants to do his part. As he walks toward Santa, who is busy trying to find and then read the misplaced "good boys and girls" list, a "soft red glow" provides light like a lantern. Realizing what an asset Rudolph will be, Santa places him at the head of the sleigh team.

Of the three books, the Little Golden Books version of *Rudolph* seems to have circulated most widely, becoming a replacement for the original. The other two sequels seem to have never really caught on. The readers of the Little Golden Books version of *Rudolph* (like myself) would grow up with no knowledge of the original. It also must have seemed odd that while the book still carried May's stamp, permissions were obtained from Marks for the prose that mimicked parts of the song. While *Rudolph* continued to reach a large audience, he seemed further and further from his historical roots.

While a child would have read—or had a parent read—these books at home, they were also read at schools during the holiday season and borrowed from the public library. A December 9, 1952, article in Michigan's *Ludington Daily News* states, "Mrs. Ruby Wanamaker's second grade have begun singing Christmas songs and listening to Christmas stories, . . . Recently, they listened to a recording of 'Rudolph's Second Christmas.'"[5] In an article from 1961, the reader is informed that the Owosso, Michigan, Public Library had just acquired recordings of *Rudolph the Red-Nosed Reindeer* and *Rudolph's Second Christmas*.[6] Rudolph was everywhere.

Comic Books and Strips by Rube Grossman

While we tend to view the 1940s and 1950s as an era of innocence, cultural critics and parents at the time worried greatly over the impact of popular culture on children. At various times, parents became alarmed at comic books, rock and roll, and television. Fears were also frequently wrapped up in issues of class, race, and sexuality—worries that white, middle-class children would be tainted by the world outside. While many of these fears focused on teenagers (juvenile delinquency, for instance), it became evident that even the smallest children had access to popular culture without adult filters.

In the late 1940s and early 1950s, horror and crime comic books became quite controversial. Dr. Fredric Wertham played the leading role in the comic scare, writing articles and a book that revealed what he viewed as the depravity of the industry: "Comic books are the greatest book publishing success in history and the greatest mass influence on children. If I make the most conservative estimate from my own researches, one billion times a year a child sits down and reads a comic book. Crime does not pay, but crime comics do."[7] The most infamous comic books were published by EC—William Gaines's Entertainment Comics—and included *Tales from the Crypt*. Perhaps the most familiar image today of the EC era features a man holding the head of a woman in one hand and an ax in the other. When the U.S. Senate investigated the comic book industry, this image received attention. Asked at a Senate subcommittee hearing whether he believed this cover to be in good taste, Gaines answered: "Yes sir; I do, for the cover of a horror comic. A cover in bad taste, for example, might be defined as holding the head a little higher so that the neck could be seen dripping blood from it and moving the body over a little further so that the neck of the body could be seen to be bloody."[8] One imagines that Gaines's statement only reaffirmed Wertham's critique of the industry. Critics initiated a moral crusade to clean up the comics industry, eventually leading to the self-policing Comics Code Authority in the fall of 1954. While controversy remained, many of the most offensive comics disappeared (including all of EC's, save *Mad*).

Seemingly, *Santa Claus Funnies* and *The Brand-New Adventures of Rudolph the Red-Nosed Reindeer* were the kind of comic books that no parent would have to worry about. Like *Donald Duck* or other Disney titles, these comics were designed as family entertainment. But even *Rudolph* comic books—starting in 1955—received the Comics Code Authority seal of approval on the front cover. For Mom and Dad reading the lurid reports of comic books and juvenile delinquency, the seal of approval worked as shorthand: even if they no longer read along with the child, as they had with May's original, they could rest assured that these brand-new adventures of Rudolph were suitable for Junior and Sis.

Even with the controversy, the market for comic books proved as massive as that of children's records. In the early 1950s, children were purchasing sixty million copies of comic books per month.[9] LeRoy Ashby noted that among the youngest readers who would have bought and read *Rudolph* comic books, "95 percent of boys and 91 percent of girls read comics."[10] Ashby also noted that even while comics may have been controversial, they "generally mirrored the triumphalist consensus of the early Cold War. American institutions and values reigned supreme."[11] *Rudolph* comic books had no intention of rocking the mainstream boat.

Rudolph story lines proliferated in newspapers and comic books during the 1950s. In newspapers (at least between 1951 and 1956) *Rudolph* appeared in a comic strip featured between Thanksgiving and Christmas. For the DC comic books, one *Rudolph* issue would be printed each year during the Christmas season between 1950 and 1961. A 1962 issue mostly reprinted a number of earlier stories (one series seems to be an adaptation from an earlier newspaper series). The illustrator Rube Grossman was involved in both series. The newspaper strip was simply titled *Rudolph the Red-Nosed Reindeer* and ran in black and white; the comic book was titled *The Brand-New Adventures of Rudolph the Red-Nosed Reindeer* and was illustrated in vibrant primary colors. In at least some of these years, in the middle of November a newspaper would print a teaser for the coming comic strip: "The daily strip will take you through the hectic last days of preparation for the great event. You'll worry along with Santa and his helpers as they gather the tops and gifts together and share with them the relief of finding a way to get the gifts to the world's children on a 'foggy Christmas Eve.'"[12] The strip was distributed by King Features Syndicate.

It would be easy to imagine kids who had come of age with copies of May's *Rudolph* now graduating to comic books and strips during the early 1950s. The primary audience, then, probably consisted of young readers, six to eleven or twelve, both boys and girls.

1950–1951

The first *Rudolph* comic was issued by DC in 1950, illustrated by Rube Grossman. The issue introduces a series of characters, many of whom reappear in the other issues and also in the comic strip. J. Baddy Bear, quite clearly, is the bad guy, while Grover Groundhog is Rudolph's smart-aleck sidekick. A more grown-up and occasionally stern Santa Claus makes an appearance along with Winky and Blinky, two comic, clumsy elves. Most of the story—though the plot is quite rudimentary—takes place at the North Pole, where Rudolph lives. His parents and home as portrayed in the original Ward's booklet are never mentioned.

If May's original *Rudolph* is a coming-of-age story, the first *Brand-New Adventure* focuses on an obvious change in Rudolph's world: he is now famous. Everywhere he goes, forest creatures ask for his help; he shines a light into a log so that a squirrel can find an acorn. Rudolph, though, seems unaware of his new fame: it seems like a purely local phenomenon. Because Orville the Owl needs to wear sunglasses to protect his eyes from the red nose, Rudolph promises to let him know whenever he comes around. Rudolph, a celebrity at the North Pole, remains the same humble, helpful reindeer he has always been.

Or at least he does until Judy and Jack, two children, show up at the North Pole. He learns that he is famous *everywhere*, and that he is featured "on radio— and television—and we sing songs about you—everything!"[13] This leads to a great deal of daydreaming on Rudolph's part, producing a subpar effort in the toy workshop; Rudolph paints toys as absentmindedly as Hermey the Elf will fourteen years later. He pays so little attention to what he is doing that he paints

*The Brand-New Adventures of Rudolph the
Red-Nosed Reindeer* (back cover), 1950

*The Brand-New Adventures of Rudolph the
Red-Nosed Reindeer* (cover), 1950

Winky the Elf, who calls him a "clumsy fool!"[14] Rudolph gets angry and insists he does not need to work like everyone else; he is famous, after all. From here, everything goes downhill fast for our big-headed hero.

In short order Rudolph's behavior gets him marked off of Santa's sleigh team for Christmas. Curiously, after Rudolph's confrontation with Santa, other reindeer are shown—once again—making fun of him. No one seems to learn anything in these narratives. Finally, he believes that no one appreciates him, leading him to run away from the dormitory where he lives with the other lead reindeer. From here, Rudolph has one mishap after another, until he finally learns his lesson. Santa rescues him on Christmas Eve, and Rudolph—since it is a clear night—simply sits on the back of the sleigh, working as a tail light in case airplanes get too near.

For Rudolph's initial foray into comics, his creators played it safe. On the whole, Rudolph's adventures are more episodic than plotted, while the outcome is fairly predictable. A couple of components, however, prove more satisfying. While Rudolph remains a young reindeer, the comic book is clearly meant for slightly older children than was the original Ward's promotion. Whereas the rhyming meter of the original invited parents to read to younger children, the new adventures were probably something a boy or girl of eight or nine or ten would read on his or her own. The most surprising element of the comic, though, is the self-referential story line.

Instead of treating Rudolph as a comic book character in a comic book world, the storyline expresses a self-awareness of Rudolph's recent fame. A character named Rudolph, featured in a popular book and perhaps even more popular song, became a cultural icon in 1949–50. A character named Rudolph is literally, within American popular culture, famous, and the 1950 comic book recognizes this. Interestingly, this story line ditches Rudolph's original timeline: while his first flight was in 1939, the comic book suggests it took place in 1949, when Gene Autry's version of Johnny Marks's song became a huge hit.

In the first newspaper comic strip from 1951, the plot seems to have been partly borrowed from the first comic book (1950). Santa Claus is gone, and the busy elves have grown surly, so Rudolph decides that he—the most famous reindeer

of all—should take charge. Grover Groundhog makes a fairly safe prediction when he says, "This is going to be bad!"[15] Quickly, the elves react to Rudolph's bossiness by quitting, leaving the toy shop with no one to run it and only a month until Christmas. When Santa's shadow appears in the doorway and he shouts "Rudolph!" he looks like a character who just stepped out of an EC horror comic.

One aspect that seems rather disturbing in these comics is how hard Rudolph and the others must work to make sure children will have toys. At one point, Rudolph is completely worn out on a treadmill and Grover congratulates him on breaking a new production record. At another point Rudolph's nose has been hooked to failing generators, providing power but leaving him, once again, exhausted. Making toys at the North Pole really does not seem like much fun.

The Brand-New Adventures of Rudolph the Red-Nosed Reindeer, cover (left), back cover (middle), and insert (right), 1951

Playing It Safe with Reindeer Games

The plots of these comic strips and books grew thinner over time, perhaps revealing the structural limitations of the set-up. One often noted feature of the 1964 Rankin/Bass version of *Rudolph* is how the bad guy (the Bumble) is reformed.

Reforming the bad guys (Baddy Bear, Black Beard, and Uncle Bigby) also happens in almost every winter issue of *Rudolph*, even if the characters revert to being bad by the beginning of the next comic. Even when these characters are doing bad things—attempting to outshine Rudolph, trying to stop Christmas, etc.—they never seem that bad. Because of this, the plots of these comic books have very little drama.

Strangely, in more than one issue (but by no means in the majority), Santa Claus becomes the most abrasive character. At times his anger seems justified, as when Rudolph—his ego growing once again—tells Santa how to improve his North Pole operation. At other times, though, Santa is impatient, surly, and blames other characters for things that were not their fault. He can also be a difficult taskmaster. One odd feature for a children's comic relates to work in Santa's toy factory. In many of the plots, Rudolph and others must pitch in at the last minute and work extra hard to finish up the toys. Toy production often seems more like factory work than the kind of thing that happy elves complete. Besides his main job on Christmas Eve, then, Santa Claus is foreman, as well as father figure and friend, to Rudolph, the elves, and Grover.

Also, to repeat an earlier observation, Rudolph is never allowed to grow up or even grow. Like in a sitcom, everything returns to the starting point at the beginning of each new issue. Even if Rudolph learned to be more modest in the 1950 issue, he has the same problem in the 1956 issue. There may be new ways to use his nose (as radar; as a super-heater; as a rope cutter), but everything else remains unchanged.

Despite what might seem like aesthetic limitations to a scholar, it is doubtful that many of the readers of *Rudolph* comics in real time shared these same concerns. While cultural critics certainly made their impact on the comic book industry during the early 1950s, sales remained robust, and comics were literally everywhere in a child's life. As May's original *Rudolph* was distributed in some schools, comic books about everything from science (GE's "Adventures in Electricity") to history (M. Philip Copp's "Eight Great Americans") circulated widely.

Also, for the youngest of these young readers, *The Brand-New Adventures of Rudolph* would have been a great investment in all things Christmas. For these readers, Rudolph would have been mythic, just like Santa Claus. As May's wife Virginia said of the May children, "First of all the children in their babyhood believed in Rudolph just as implicitly as they did in Santa Claus."[16] And while Rudolph was clearly a commercial-culture product, children invested a great deal of effort in consuming him. Children bought *Rudolph* at ten cents an issue, read and reread each issue, and traded copies with other kids. Each issue also

Robert L. May and Rube Grossman, *Rensdyret Rudolf med den røde tud* (the Danish adaptation of *Rudolph the Red-Nosed Reindeer*), circa 1950s (second page) | Papers of Robert L. May, Rauner Special Collections Library, Dartmouth College; courtesy of Dartmouth College Library

included a number of games and puzzles; there was no advertising. With the newspaper comics, children sometimes cut out and saved the strips. One newspaper offered free scrapbooks. "Boys and girls can make their own Rudolph comic books by clipping and coloring the daily cartoon strips and pasting them in the scrapbook."[17] It was also possible that the youngest readers of *The Brand-New Adventures of Rudolph* treated these comics as sources for real information. As James Barnett wrote in 1954: "Because simple illustrated stories about Christmas are now available at low cost, children are likely to gain comprehension of it increasingly from each other. Each age group will tend to learn from the next older one and to spread such knowledge laterally to its members."[18] Ironically, the "safe" comic books also seemed to remove Mom and Dad from the picture of holiday folklore.

Low-Flying Reindeer

The Brand-New Adventures of Rudolph and the *Rudolph* comic strip seemed tailor-made for the baby boom generation. As adults worried over juvenile delinquency, horror comics, and rock and roll, Rudolph remained a comforting icon that parents easily accepted as safe. The last new adventure would be issued in 1961, a sign that Rudolph's cultural popularity *and* relevance no longer burned as bright as they had in 1951. While Dr. Wertham continued to rail against comics, in the end the lack of a new Gene Autry to introduce "Rudolph" to a new set of baby boomers probably set the series into decline. After 1954, May wrote no other sequels, leaving the Little Golden Books *Rudolph* to be *the* Rudolph, at least for a few years.

While *Rudolph* would fly a bit lower during the latter part of the 1950s, he remained a familiar cultural icon. Ward's still sold Rudolph toys, and homeowners, unable to find Rudolph lawn decorations, put red noses on Comet and Cupid. Still, Rudolph was an icon that paid only part of the bills. May, writing to Dartmouth in 1958, noted,

> Aside from obituaries, we'd say a class secretary's most difficult writing occurs when he's forced to report something about himself. (For this item, we'll drop the "secretarial we"!) After seven years of self-employment, ending in two years of unintended semi-retirement, I've returned to Montgomery Ward, as Promotional Editor of their catalogs. (One of the company's slogans: "Ward's will take anything back!") Some of you may recall that I was with Ward's for fifteen years, till Rudolph whisked me away in '51. But Rudolph's been flying slower and slower these last few years . . . so I was very happy to accept Ward's offer. An unbalanced budget and deficit spending may or may not be sound at the National level . . . but at the home level, believe me, they're both unsound and unpleasant![19]

eight
A NEW CHRISTMAS
TRADITION

As Rudolph approached his fifteenth birthday, one of Robert May's daughters asked him a difficult question: Did Rudolph really exist?

> I knew she wanted me to say "yes," but how could I? All of the good things that have happened to us are because of Rudolph and she was sure to learn sometime. I had to tell her the truth, but I still left the answer open.
>   "Well, Daddy made up Rudolph before you were born, but maybe Santa Claus liked the idea and got a real one."[1]

May's dilemma, in fact, was little different from when to tell a child the truth about Santa Claus. Still, there were primary differences between Santa and Rudolph, partly rooted in the historical past.

The origins of an American Santa Claus dated back to the 1820s, over a hundred years before the birth of Rudolph in 1939. Scholars labeled Santa Claus as an invented American tradition, finding little evidence of his European roots in Clement C. Moore's "A Visit from St. Nicholas" of 1823. Still, the elapsed time buried these origins in mystery and half-truths, leaving the *impression* of folklore. This impression was also supported by a simple fact: no one owned Santa Claus's image. Advertisers made use of Santa to sell everything from toothpaste to cigarettes, but no one could copyright the red suit or reindeer or North Pole residence. As Dad donned whiskers, Mom read "A Visit from St. Nicholas" to Junior and Sis, and kids left cookies and milk as gifts on Christmas Eve, the lore of Santa continued to shape itself into a recognizable form. In this way, Santa became a piece of Americana so familiar that no line could be drawn between him and Christmas.

Rudolph, on the other hand, had a specific author and date of birth: Robert L. May had created Rudolph for Montgomery Ward in 1939. While Santa would be usurped by Coca-Cola and others over time, Rudolph—from his very inception—had always been a commercial animal. He had been created by a copywriter for the primary purpose of increasing store traffic for Montgomery Ward during the holiday season. Indeed, at every important juncture in Rudolph's life, he would receive support from big business. In the late 1940s, even as May took ownership of Rudolph's copyright, Ward's continued to promote the red-nosed reindeer heavily, including financing the first animated version of *Rudolph* in 1948. In the late 1940s and early 1950s, Columbia Records helped turn Gene Autry's recording of "Rudolph" into a massive hit. And in 1963–64, GE provided the funds for Rankin/Bass's animated *Rudolph the Red-Nosed Reindeer*. For every Rudolph toy sold, for every Gene Autry record played on the radio, and for every animated special aired on network television, someone made a profit. Born as a copyright, Rudolph has remained one ever since.

Rudolph suffered the same contradictions as Mickey, Donald, and many other media-made stars. He was a folk hero without folk origins, a children's fable born of commercial culture. Even as Rudolph became ingrained as part of Christmas tradition, these contradictions would continue to define how Americans would experience him.

A New Christmas Tradition (James Barnett)

As Rudolph soared to new heights during the early 1950s, he received unexpected attention from academia. James H. Barnett, working on a book about Christmas in America, described Rudolph as the "only original addition to the folklore of

Santa Claus in this century."[2] In his research, Barnett corresponded with and interviewed Robert May (this material has not survived). As a result of his research and inquiries, Barnett would offer the first in-depth look at Rudolph as part of American Christmas lore.

In his analysis in *The American Christmas*, Barnett begins with, "The tale of Rudolph the Red-Nosed Reindeer is a very important addition to the folk celebration of Christmas."[3] One aspect of Rudolph that we lose track of today is how quickly he established himself as a central part of an American Christmas. *Rudolph* was introduced by Montgomery Ward in 1939, temporarily retired during World War II, and reintroduced by Ward's in 1946; and in 1949 "Rudolph the Red-Nosed Reindeer" became a massive hit. Even as Rudolph celebrated his tenth anniversary in 1949, he had been promoted for only five of those years (1939, 1946, 1947, 1948, and 1949). Despite the ebb and flow, Rudolph—in a few short years—had become a recognizable and accepted symbol of an American Christmas.

Rudolph's acceptance carried a depth that separated him from other popular cultural icons, whether Christmas related (Frosty the Snowman) or not (Popeye). The phenomenon of Rudolph had grown beyond the fact that kids read about him in comic books or listened to songs about him. Kids and parents viewed Rudolph as a permanent addition to Santa's entourage. From a historical point of view, this growth was phenomenal. If an American Santa Claus had taken a hundred years to attain his modern persona, then Rudolph was on an accelerated path: he would accomplish nearly the same thing in fifteen years.

Barnett alludes to two other points that have often been overlooked, perhaps because they seem obvious. Rudolph is a completely secular Christmas myth. Even more to the point, Rudolph has become intertwined in the most popular secular, holiday tradition: the Santa Claus myth. As with "A Visit from St. Nicholas," which May mimicked, the original *Rudolph* story never introduces religious imagery. To Barnett, this supports a general trend in which modern media (records, comics, and films) primarily support a secular vision of Christmas. From a commercial point of view, aligning Rudolph with religious symbols would have only limited his appeal. Like "White Christmas" or *Miracle on 34th Street*, Rudolph's story and personality had to draw from a pool of holiday symbols (reindeer, Santa Claus) that would appeal to all Americans.

Another factor that might seem obvious is that May chose a reindeer for his story. Reindeer, of course, had already been a part of the Christmas story since 1821–22, which guaranteed the choice of animal would be familiar to children. Barnett wrote: "By way of explanation, it should be noted that the reindeer has long been a favorite animal figure in the United States. In addition to its magical associations already established by Moore's poem, it is a creature with which children can identify themselves."[4] In fact, May had taken a familiar element and, dramatically and philosophically, improved on it: Rudolph became the only reindeer who stands out as an individual.

This also speaks to the difference between the original *Rudolph* and Moore's "A Visit from St. Nicholas." While both poems focus on the Christmas experience, May shifts his point of view to incorporate more contemporary ideas on children. Obviously, May has chosen an animal to write about, adding a fabulist note that probably makes the magic more believable. But this is unimportant when measuring the differences between the two poems. In "A Visit from St. Nicholas," we meet the children who are snug in their beds, dreaming of sugarplums. Strangely, perhaps, for a poem so beloved by children, this is the last time children appear in the poem. The narrative is focused on an adult literally describing St. Nicholas's visit. In *Rudolph*, however, the opposite happens. The poem remains focused on Rudolph himself, the child, from beginning to end. Everything in the story—even Santa Claus—serves as a backdrop to highlight Rudolph. May has borrowed from tradition but also updated it. Children are no longer content to just hear a story about Santa Claus: they now wish to be in the center of it.

One of Barnett's sharpest observations concerned Santa Claus himself. Traditionally, Santa has been shown with godlike powers, allowing him to observe children's behavior, fly with his sleigh and magical reindeer, and deliver toys to all the children in the world in one night. In Rudolph's story, however, Santa seems as powerless in the face of weather and air traffic as anyone else. In May's original,

Santa and his reindeer team become entangled in a tree and nearly crash into an airplane. Simply put, Santa's eyesight fails to penetrate the fog, and his inability to navigate threatens to prevent him from completing his most important job: delivering toys to boys and girls. Instead of seeming magical, this new, more human Santa Claus struggled with everyday problems.

Without omniscient powers, Santa needed someone like Rudolph to complete his journey. "Symbolically, the small child came to the aid of the powerful parents and exhibited unexpected powers. . . . To some degree, the possibility that children identify with Rudolph offers an explanation of the sudden and continuing popularity of the story, the song, and the various pictorial representations of this now-famous deer."[5] The child, identifying with Rudolph, gets to come to the rescue of adults like Santa Claus.

Barnett also calls attention to how closely Rudolph's story mimics the American success myth. Rudolph not only gets to join Santa's team; he becomes—while still no more than a young deer—the lead reindeer. Once given the chance, he exceeds expectations, winning fame (if not fortune) in the process. "Rudolph seems to express an important theme of American culture through his success in becoming the *lead* reindeer of Santa's team, which may not be unrelated to the American faith in every person's ability to succeed if he can only 'get a break.'"[6]

Barnett closes his section on Rudolph with a cautionary note, focusing on a lingering question. "It remains to be seen if the Rudolph tale will survive the annual orgy of exploitation in pre-Christmas advertising."[7] Barnett's focus on Christmas advertising underlined a problem at the heart of Rudolph: he straddled the folk-commercial fault line. While few scholars followed Barnett in his study of Rudolph and Christmas, many turned their attention to this commercial-folk divide. Rudolph's origin in commercial culture was hardly unique in the 1930s and 1940s. The popularization of American folklore had made it more difficult to draw a line between Disney's Paul Bunyan and logging tales collected by a professional. As the 1950s began, this distinction held the attention of American folklorists.

Folklore and Fakelore

In 1950, a time when intellectuals openly battled over ideas, Richard Dorson started an academic food fight over the issue of authenticity in folklore. What set off Dorson was the popular use of folklore. Popular writers, claiming to represent authentic folk culture, were cashing in on fluffy Paul Bunyan and John Henry stories. Because these stories, according to Dorson, had no roots in American soil, because most of them had been made up out of whole cloth, he dubbed them "fakelore."

By the time Dorson got around to writing "Folklore and Fake Lore" for the *American Mercury* in March 1950, he no longer approached the subject politely. "Far from fulfilling its high promise, the study [of folklore] has been falsified, abused and exploited, and the public deluded with Paul Bunyan nonsense and claptrap collections."[8] Dorson, however, was just getting warmed up: "These comic demigods are not products of a native mythology, but rather of a chauvinist and fascist conception of folklore. They must be 100 per cent native American supermen, all-conquering, all-powerful, braggart and whimsically destructive. By such distorted folk symbols the Nazis supported their thesis of a Nordic super-race, and touted Hitler as their greatest folklorist."[9] Strong words, no doubt. The problem of fakelore was made worse by the fact that authors sold it to Americans as the real thing. Publishers, looking only at the bottom line, promoted books like *Paul Bunyan of the Great Lakes* as the genuine article.

This self-created folklore/fakelore became even more problematic when centered on business mascots—Keebler's elves, McDonald's Ronald, and Ward's Rudolph—primarily designed to offer a friendly face to win over the consumer. Here, even the idea of folk roots had disappeared, becoming, in one scholar's estimate, fakelure: commercial culture mimicking folklore.

Dorson's argument was easily brought to bear on the evolution of Santa Claus. Originally, various Europeans settled in America, bringing holiday customs to the New World. Instead of Santa Claus, for instance, the Germans brought the fur-clad Belsnickle, who accompanied Saint Nicholas on gift-giving rounds. The Christ Child (Christkindl), also from Germany, delivered presents on a donkey.

In early American settlements, these various, low-key traditions thrived separately in isolated communities, mostly in the Northeast (Pennsylvania, New York). Even the day of the gift giver's arrival varied widely (December 6, 24, and 31).[10] These traditions surely qualified as true Christmas folklore. The idea of one gift giver, dressed in red and white, would evolve only over time.

By the early nineteenth century, however, these local traditions faded into the background as a number of writers created and promoted a new "tradition" that owed very little to European folklore. Individuals like Washington Irving and Clement C. Moore began to self-consciously use folklore to create a new American tradition. Stephen Nissenbaum noted: "Nowadays, many Americans believe, as I did until recently, that there was nothing new about 'the night before Christmas' described in Moore's poem—that the story it told was simply an old Dutch tradition brought to the New World in the seventeenth century and then, in the natural course of things, gradually Americanized. . . . Instead, the familiar Santa Claus story appears to have been devised in the early nineteenth century, during the two decades that ended in the early 1820s."[11] As Irving drew from the Dutch tradition in New York, he had Saint Nicholas exchange his churchly origin for a clay pipe and Dutch clothing. Moore's influence—thanks to "A Visit from St. Nicholas"—would be even more keenly felt. During these early decades of the nineteenth century, Irving's and Moore's work helped crystallize the idea of an American Santa Claus.

Drawing from the historical evidence, Dorson wrote, "This image of the plump, jolly old fellow in the red coat and cap dropping down the chimney with a bag full of presents is purely an American creation."[12] Irving and Moore fashioned, as an "invented tradition," an early example of fakelore.[13]

One caveat should be added to these observations. While both Irving and Moore clearly bent the rules of folklore, their innovations still—looking back— seem fairly innocent. One man wished to kick-start the idea of an old-fashioned Christmas; the other wished for no more than to amuse children. The fakelore, in this instance, lacked the money motive that Dorson saw in those who made fakelore popular in his own day.

A hundred years later all bets were off and Santa had clearly become a piece of folk*lure*, a commercially driven symbol. As James Twitchell wrote, "You can keep Christ out of Christmas, but not Coke's Santa."[14] Starting in 1931, Coca-Cola used Haddon Sundblom's brightly illustrated drawings of Santa Claus in magazine advertisements, on highway billboards, and for in-store displays. These ads seem to have been particularly effective during the 1930s and 1940s, a time when full-blown color layouts in magazines like *Life* were still rare. On the page, these ads popped. They also featured what Twitchell referred to as Coca-Cola's "corporate colors." "He is working out of Atlanta"—Coca-Cola headquarters—Twitchell wrote, "not out of the North Pole."[15] Each ad featured a larger-than-life Santa, saturated with warm reds and plush whites, and seeking the soft drink that refreshes. While the ads borrowed freely from Santa lore, they were designed with one purpose: to sell Coca-Cola.

Within folklore, Santa Claus had a real past, however obscure. But in the view of a folklorist like Dorson, the celebration of that past had been tainted by the self-conscious use of custom and finally perverted by the introduction of the profit motive. Still, a folk aspect remained, because many celebrated Santa Claus outside the marketplace. The question was, could the same be said of Rudolph? Was he purely a commercial creature, bought and paid for by those who legally owned his image? Was he a new kind of folklore, born of commercial culture but still capable of superseding it? Or was Rudolph something in between, a consumable product at a store near you *and* a myth that enriched the childhood experience of Christmas?

Rudolph as Folk

From a purist's point of view, Rudolph would be able to claim no more than a thread of folklore from Christmas past. He was a reindeer, even if his pictorial representation more closely represented Bambi than a baby caribou. And although reindeer were creatures clearly connected to Santa Claus and Christmas, Moore and others may have invented this tradition. Barnett wrote, "There is no scholarly authority for the idea that he [Santa Claus] came in a reindeer-drawn sleigh."[16] Even this thread meant little, however, because Rudolph had been cut out whole cloth by an advertising man working for a giant retail store. For the purist, Rudolph only borrowed the allure of folklore for commercial ends. This logic, however, had one flaw: many people, and especially children, embraced Rudolph as genuine folklore.

Even while Rudolph's folk roots were probably nonexistent, his popularity overflowed his commercial origins. When newspaper columnists mentioned Rudolph during the 1950s and early 1960s, they knew that their readers would understand the reference. Under the headline of "What to Do If Cold Gives Nose a Glow," Eleanor Nangle wrote, "Rudolph the reindeer is more than welcome to that red nose of his. Nobody else wants one."[17] In the "Voice of Youth Column" in the *Chicago Tribune*, sixteen-year-old Camilla Schmalz wrote a letter ("Dear Boys and Girls") explaining how Rudolph's nose became red. After a mishap in a storeroom (Rudolph was attempting to look at his Christmas present early), he was covered with the contents of a bucket of red paint. Santa Claus brought a bottle of turpentine to clean up Rudolph, but the paint on his nose stubbornly remained.[18] And the Bosen Costume Company, busy tailoring Santa suits, added a Rudolph "headpiece which has a battery driven light in the nose."[19]

While folk references like these could be funny and off the cuff, many settings encouraged children to interact with Rudolph as they might with Santa Claus at the local mall. In a series of pictures for the *Los Angeles Examiner* in 1951, Santa Claus is seen greeting children in an orthopedic hospital in California. "Santa Claus brought one of his trusted helpers with him yesterday, Rudolph, the famous red-nosed reindeer, when he visited children at the Orthopedic Hospital."[20] In one photograph Santa is shown interacting with three children, and clearly he would have—traditionally—been the most anticipated surprise. Better yet, though, Santa, on this trip, traveled with Rudolph himself!

It is impossible, of course, to know what each child thought of this presentation, but two general interpretations can be offered. First, these children, even with limited access to outside media, were probably quite familiar with Rudolph. In

Santa visits the Christmas party at the orthopedic hospital in Los Angeles, sponsored by the Juniors of the League for Crippled Children, 1951 | Courtesy of University of Southern California, on behalf of the USC Libraries Special Collections

1951, the year of these pictures, Red Foley charted with "Rudolph," while the animated *Rudolph the Red-Nosed Reindeer* continued to circulate. The Maxton edition of *Rudolph*, along with a new pop-up *Rudolph* in 1950, also crowded Christmas stockings and public library shelves. Second, the idea of Rudolph, both then and now, was perhaps quite real for young children. Like Santa Claus, many children may have considered Rudolph less a fantasy than a fact of holiday life. Whether they believed a deer from the local zoo was Rudolph or not, many still believed in the reality of Rudolph. "Children are less mystified and amazed about Christmas customs than adult perception would predict," wrote Cindy Dell Clark. "For the most part, children take their faith in stride."[21]

In a third picture, a boy bends forward to get a better look. The deer, more closely resembling a white-tail deer than a caribou calf, seems more distracted by the camera flash than the attention of the children. The cage has been placed very close to the children, whose faces can be seen through the wire on the other side of the cage. The bespectacled Santa is pointing at the cage, perhaps explaining something about Rudolph to the children. The fact that Santa showed up with Rudolph on December 22, two days before his Christmas Eve deliveries, must have made the showing even more impressive.

Christmas at Butler Brothers at Lakewood Park, California, 1951 . . . Rudolph's nose catches on fire | Courtesy of University of Southern California, on behalf of the USC Libraries Special Collections,

Another Rudolph story, in the same paper on the same day, had a more humorous slant:

> "Help! Santa Claus, bring the first aid kit and a fire extinguisher. Rudolph is in trouble." Yes, Rudolph the red-nosed reindeer was really red hot. In fact, the rosey proboscis which has made Rudolph the most famous of all reindeer, was on fire. You see, it all happened while Rudolph was making a pre-Christmas appearance atop Butler Brother's department store in Lakewood Park (California). Rudolph was the

victim of sabotage when a short circuit started a fire in his sniffer which in this case [w]as a large red light bulb. Passers by, including a few worried youngsters, were startled when Rudolph gave out a miniature explosion amid a shower of sparks and smoke. No serious damage resulted, except possibly to Rudolph's dignity, and Santa Claus, who left his post in the toy department to help extinguish the blaze which was confined to Rudolph, said the animal, red nose and all would be back in shape in time to help him make his Christmas deliveries.[22]

While this happening may have the air of a staged publicity stunt, no doubt the department store thought it worthwhile to have a Rudolph with an electronic red nose.

While borrowing deer from the local zoo to accompany Santa Claus to hospitals and shopping malls may seem unusual today (and humanely questionable), live deer were quite common in Christmas settings during this period.

Even after the Rudolph juggernaut had slowed considerably during the early 1960s, his cultural resonance remained. On December 24, 1961, James T. Carter of the *Victoria Advocate*, in Texas, penned a story titled "Real Deer with Nose That Glows": "This true Christmas story of a living 'Rudolph, the Red Nosed Reindeer' doesn't begin anywhere near the North Pole or even near Christmastime. It actually begins on the Guadalupe River a few miles southwest of Placedo at a time last June when the river was a torrent of flood-waters."[23] From the bank of the surging river, eleven-year-old Buster Hafer spotted a young buck in danger of drowning. "I was looking for anything to catch him by," Buster related, "and what I finally caught hold of were his ears."[24] "Bambi" joined the menagerie of animals back home, including horses, a dog, and chickens. When Christmastime arrived, however, Bambi—known to Buster's classmates—got a role of a lifetime: the Christmas pageant needed a Rudolph, and Bambi fit the mold. "I don't mind Bambi being Rudolph," Buster said; "It's that lipstick on his nose." Rudolph went into rehearsals, and "one of the teachers who shall be nameless here volunteered

The Rudolph statue
that Robert May kept
on his lawn at Christ-
mastime | Papers
of Robert L. May,
Rauner Special Col
lections Library, Dart-
mouth College; cour-
tesy of Dartmouth
College Library

the use of her cherry-red lipstick for the tip of Bambi's nose." Carter continues: "And it sort of left a cherry-red glow over the whole town of Placedo, whence came this true Christmas story for Christmas Eve."[25]

Much later (1984), columnist Paul Jones recalled an accidental visit by Rudolph on Christmas Eve at a children's hospital in northern Wisconsin:

As one little guy gazed out the window near his bed, he saw a wonderful sight: A deer—a *real* deer—was standing in the snow and looking at him!

"It's Rudolph!" he cried, and, since he could walk, he climbed out of bed, opened a fire door . . . , and in walked the deer. His nose wasn't red, but who cares for details at a time like this? Here was Rudolph on Christmas Eve, and what could be more appropriate.[26]

While Rudolph would be captured and returned to the wild by the hospital staff, he had, during his brief visit, given "a ward full of sick and lonely children . . . the thrill of their lives."[27]

Around 1950 May got into the folk-image act himself with a little help from a friendly manufacturer who created a giant Rudolph, variously described as an eight- or nine-foot statue, which May placed on his lawn. A *Chicago Tribune* article from 1972 noted: "For the last 23 years at Christmastime, a giant model of Rudolph has glowed on the lawn at May's home. He has no idea how many children have had their pictures taken sitting on his 'son's' back."[28] Illuminated by a floodlight, the statue remained a living legacy to "the house Rudolph built."

A New American Tradition

Because we have lived with Rudolph so long, perhaps the folklore/fakelore dispute seems beside the point. Children, Rudolph's biggest fans, often see him as real, making the question of his origins meaningless. Parents read May's *Rudolph* to their children or have their children photographed with the book, experiencing the myth away from consumer culture. Whatever the reason for Rudolph's creation, it has little to do with how children and parents experience him in the home at Christmastime. This line of reasoning, however, excludes quite a bit. No one would argue that Rudolph was anything less than a popular folk hero, but there remain a couple of issues worth considering.

The first revolves around Rudolph's popularity. The real problem with measuring Rudolph's popularity—his mythic resonance as a pop-folk hero—is that he has never been allowed to develop in an organic setting. In traditional folk societies, a song or story would grow out of that culture, and its continued use signified its relevance. With Rudolph, businesses with vast resources created and promoted his image to further their economic goals. With these businesses always pumping up Rudolph as a symbol, it becomes difficult to separate publicity from an authentic response. Ward's first two Rudolph campaigns in 1939 and 1946 underline this problem.

Boy with Rudolph book (found photograph) | Courtesy of Suzanne Tate

"Mailsters on Parade," representing Santa's reindeer. The lead mailster's buggy has a red light (Smithsonian Institution, 1954)

Nearly every magazine story about Ward's and *Rudolph the Red-Nosed Reindeer* repeats that millions of copies were given away in 1939 and 1946, equating the six million books with Rudolph's popularity. Newspaper stories written at the time noted that *Rudolph*'s distribution surpassed best sellers. Much of this, however, was just smart publicity. Millions of copies of *Rudolph* had moved from Ward's counters to children's stockings, and undoubtedly thousands of children embraced May's "Ugly Duckling" story. But *Rudolph*, from the start, had one primary goal: to promote Ward's economic well-being. Copies of *Rudolph* were *given* away—a gimmick to bring families into the store for the all-important Christmas season. The cost of the booklets, like any business or promotional fee, would be calculated as part of doing business. Ward's likewise discovered the power of getting *Rudolph* into schools: each copy read to a classroom by a teacher and each copy brought home by a student worked to further publicize Ward's.

Ward's never gave away six million copies of *Rudolph* because of demand. The retail giant planned ahead in 1939 and 1946, asking for orders from individual stores to complete one mass printing of *Rudolph* in both years. These, the printed copies, were the copies that would be available. In some instances stores ran out of copies, and in other instances copies remained under the counter. *Rudolph*, no doubt, was a big hit with children, but Montgomery Ward aggressively planned to distribute the number of copies that had been printed. Instead of reacting to the demand, Ward's created it.

This promotional feat would be repeated again and again with Rudolph. Columbia pursued a special promotion for a number of its best-selling records, including Gene Autry's "Rudolph the Red-Nosed Reindeer." DC Comics, undoubtedly seeing the popularity of "Rudolph" in 1949, published the first issue of *The Brand-New Adventures of Rudolph the Red-Nosed Reindeer* in 1950. Later GE would be instrumental in the funding and promotion of Rankin/Bass's *Rudolph the Red-Nosed Reindeer* (1964). Obviously, all of these businesses spread Rudolph's fame, and undoubtedly much of the response was genuine. But there was nothing about these promotions that could be called organic.

As folklore, the ownership of Rudolph creates another thorny issue. Characters like Disney's Donald Duck and May's Rudolph often seem woven into the fabric of popular culture in America. Because of this, these characters give the impression of being public property—a Ronald McDonald statue at the McDonald's playground, Mickey Mouse on a U.S. Postal Service stamp, and Rudolph as a Hallmark decoration for the family Christmas tree. Rudolph is so familiar, children notice him most when he is *not* included in a Christmas book or movie.[29]

Rudolph's *appearance* as public property, nonetheless, is merely an appearance. When Robert May received Rudolph's copyright in 1947, he set up Rudolph the Red-Nosed Reindeer Enterprises. For each new venture, May provided permission to use Rudolph's image in exchange for a licensing fee. In 1950, for instance, the Nashua Gummed and Coated Paper Company received permission from May to manufacture "Paper Napkins, Paper Table Covers, Guest Towels, and combination sets of Napkins and Paper Table Mats to be designed with reproductions of Rudolph, the Red-Nosed Reindeer. The products will be available in stores throughout the country during the holiday season."[30] However much May believed in the ideals that Rudolph symbolized, and however much he viewed Rudolph as the friend of all children, he nonetheless used him for business profit. Whether on napkins, a View-Master reel, or a Parker pen, Rudolph would be most frequently experienced as a consumer product. Every time a Rudolph product sold, May made a percentage.

May's ownership also limited how others could use Rudolph. Without May's permission, anyone who attempted to write a story or make a film that included Rudolph would be open to a lawsuit. Even though children believed that Rudolph was an essential ingredient in the Santa Claus myth, then, it was an ingredient that could be excluded from Christmas narratives because (1) permission was required, along with (2) a fee for use. This is probably the reason that Santa Claus songs and story lines far outnumber those for Rudolph: anyone can borrow Santa's image.

Nevertheless, Rudolph had become a recognizable piece of Americana by the 1950s, beloved by children who drew no lines between Superman, John Henry, and Rudolph. Even a folklorist could have made an argument that Rudolph was genuine: with children, schools, and charities adapting Rudolph as part of Christmas pageants and public displays, he resembled authentic folk culture. In Barnett's words, Rudolph had become the first new Christmas myth to establish itself in a hundred years. But even as Rudolph achieved nearly equal footing with Santa Claus in the popular consciousness, he remained on a short leash. Rudolph the Red-Nosed Reindeer was also Rudolph the Consumable Product. Rudolph was a new kind of industrial folklore, caught between his humble story line and his ability to generate millions of dollars for his owners. While Rudolph would soar even higher during the mid-1960s, he would once again require a major corporate sponsor for the flight.

nine

RANKIN/BASS'S
RUDOLPH
THE RED-NOSED
REINDEER

In 1964 Rudolph bolstered his career by appearing in a medium that had barely existed when Robert L. May first penned his story in 1939: television. As with Gene Autry's massive hit of "Rudolph the Red-Nosed Reindeer" in 1949, Rankin and Bass's holiday special introduced May's reindeer to a new generation of American children. Older baby boomers had grown up with all things Rudolph—the original book, the 1948 animated cartoon, merchandise, comic books, View-Master reels, and recorded stories. Now, Rankin and Bass's animated special would present Rudolph to younger brothers and sisters, educating baby boomers and—in reruns—Generation X.

Massively popular from the start, *Rudolph the Red-Nosed Reindeer* quickly became a yearly ritual.

"When the Rankin/Bass animated version of the Rudolph story premiered on NBC-TV in 1964, narrated by Burl Ives," wrote Tim Hollis in *Christmas Wishes*, "the red-nosed reindeer 'went down in history' even more than he had in his earlier incarnations."[1]

Of course no one knew that the new *Rudolph* would be a big success in 1964. Rankin/Bass Productions began as Videocraft International in 1955, and the company, in 1963, lacked a lengthy track record. The animated Christmas special barely existed in 1964. *Mister Magoo's Christmas Carol*, from 1962, was an exception, and

the popular *A Charlie Brown Christmas* and *How the Grinch Stole Christmas!* only followed *Rudolph* in 1965 and 1966. No one could be certain, not Rankin/Bass, sponsor GE, nor television network NBC, that *Rudolph the Red-Nosed Reindeer* would become a staple of holiday programming.

Placing Rudolph on television also had an impact on how many people learned about his story. While both the original book and Autry's song reached many millions over a period of years, Rankin/Bass's *Rudolph* simultaneously reached multi-millions in one showing. This expanded Rudolph's commercial reach as well, providing an opportunity for advertisers to push beyond the children's market and reach the entire family. Rudolph had been a star for a long time. Rankin, Bass, and scriptwriter Romeo Muller, with a little help from GE, would make Rudolph a superstar. "So familiar have Muller's ideas become," noted Hollis, "that the show is what most people think of when they hear about Rudolph."[2]

While Rudolph officially turned twenty-five in 1964, his popularity had probably peaked in the early 1950s, a few years after Autry's hit. Little Golden Books' illustrated adaption of *Rudolph* dated back to 1958, while the Rudolph DC Comics

*A Charlie Brown
Christmas* (1965) |
CBS/Photofest

BELOW LEFT
*Mister Magoo's
Christmas Carol*
(1962) | NBC/
Photofest

BELOW RIGHT
*How the Grinch Stole
Christmas!* (1966) |
CBS/Photofest

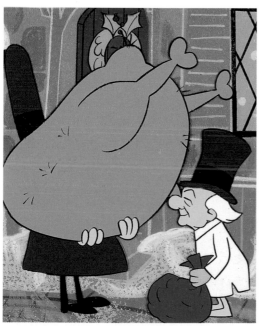

series had ceased publication in 1962. Rudolph remained an American icon, but his presence within popular culture had diminished.

Rudolph's reduced presence may have worked to Rankin/Bass's advantage. For many late baby boomers, Robert L. May and Gene Autry were distant memories. Because of this, there was less need to consider the familiar, allowing Rankin/Bass to expand on the original without upsetting expectations. Rankin/Bass, in essence, had a clean slate to reinvent Rudolph.

Still, for parents and older siblings, the outline of Rankin/Bass's *Rudolph the Red-Nosed Reindeer* remained familiar. May's story of an ugly duckling who transforms himself into a hero still served as the foundation. Rudolph's nose is still red, his playmates unfriendly, and he is unceremoniously kicked out of the reindeer games. The ending, with Santa's realization of Rudolph's true potential, likewise mirrors the original.

Almost everything in between, however, is altered considerably for Rankin/Bass's *Rudolph*. May's Rudolph lived in a house in a small village, and his parents were never named. There were no elves (though Denver Gillen's illustrations included elves with Santa at the North Pole), colorful prospectors, abominable snow monsters, or snowman narrators.

Undoubtedly, these additions to May's stories were prompted by an important consideration. The original *Rudolph* was very short. In spoken narration, it would last no longer than thirteen minutes. The Rankin/Bass special would have to fill up—with commercials—an hour of television time. For practical reasons, the story had to be expanded to fit the time, but this extension also provided a creative bonus: the Rankin/Bass team had ample room to put their stamp on the story.

Misfits in Christmastown

Like May's original book and Marks's song, Rankin/Bass's *Rudolph* has become so familiar we accept the events of the story line as completely natural. Watching it for the thirty-ninth time, submerged in the nostalgia for one's own youth, can be more like visiting an old friend. We forget, for instance, how odd it must have

The cast of *Rudolph the Red-Nosed Reindeer* (Rankin/ Bass, 1964) | NBC/ Photofest

seemed during the initial showing that an elf wanted to be a dentist. Or that a young viewer, watching Yukon fall down a crevice for the first time, does not understand that Bumbles bounce. Other things—like a very grumpy Santa and an island populated by misfits—also pass by without comment. Unselfconsciously, *Rudolph* serves as a time capsule from our own youth and a sacred memory that we pass on to our own children.

While Rudolph remains at the center of his own story, Rankin/Bass's special is almost as much about Hermey as Rudolph. Hermey, along with Rudolph, holds the moral center, and it is the journey of those two—with lots of help from Yukon Cornelius—that resolves the intergenerational cracks at the foundation of Christmastown. Hermey and Rudolph's trials and tribulations are also the heart of the story: they will do anything for a friend, including leave him behind. Set against the backdrop of old-think—following in one's father's footsteps in order to pull Santa's sleigh; building toys and liking it because that is what elves have always done—Rudolph and Hermey easily win viewers' sympathies. With the addition of Hermey and Rudolph's new friends from the Island of Misfit Toys, we have a poignant story of injustice perpetrated against those who are seen as different.

The Island of Misfit Toys serves as a secondary story, repeating and deepening the main theme. Here, it is easy to recall Robert L. May's *Rudolph's Second Christmas*, issued as an audio recording by RCA in 1951. Tim Hollis has noted the similarities between this book and the Island of Misfit Toys, and no one seems to know whether Muller was familiar with May's work or the comic book series from the 1950s and early 1960s. Whatever Muller knew, the similarities are striking, even while noting that the theme of difference is a familiar motif in children's literature. In *Rudolph's Second Christmas*, the animals Rudolph discovers have hidden themselves deep in the woods. There are

1. a turtle that runs very fast;
2. a rabbit that moves very slowly;
3. a cat that barks;
4. a dog that meows;

5. a canary that talks; and

6. a parrot that sings.

The parrot, for instance, "had never learned to say 'Polly want a cracker.'" Because the animals had been teased and rejected, they were "sad and lonely."[3] Once Rudolph puts these misfits in the circus, however, they find a place where they belong, and the circus becomes successful.

Muller's misfits are likewise isolated on the Island of Misfit Toys. Castaways, more or less, that even Santa—and this is a real sticking point—remains unaware of. Indeed, the characters seem to have created their own society, but they remain deeply unhappy: they require a child's love in order to have a purpose. This, perhaps, expands on May's original themes of rejection and isolation, allowing ample time for Charlie-in-the-Box, Dolly (the rag doll with red hair), Spotted Elephant, and others to tell their own stories. These scenes are among the most moving ones in all of *Rudolph*. If May based Rudolph on "The Ugly Duckling," the characters on the Island of Misfit Toys seem cut from the same cloth. That these toys fail to work like normal toys is not the problem; the problem is that these toys remain unloved.

This point is brought to bear when the focus rests on Dolly. As many viewers have noted, nothing seems to be wrong with her. Many years later, Rankin jokingly suggested that she had psychological problems and was under the care of an analyst. The main problem, even with nothing physically wrong, is the same as with the other misfits: she is unloved. Muller's pathos, in fact, is deeply ingrained in even the most unsuspecting of characters. The mighty Bumble, fearful enough to send shivers down the spine of Sam the Snowman, is perhaps only misunderstood or suffering from a toothache. He is, after all, alone. Once he loses his teeth and befriends Yukon, he behaves like an oversize stuffed animal.

These sympathetic souls stand out even more because the world around them—the Elf Workshop, the Reindeer Games, and the larger World Outside (for the misfit toys)—proves unfair and unkind. Rudolph's father is cruel, Santa Claus is nonsupportive, and the Elf Foreman overbearing. Even King Moon Racer, kindhearted enough to collect the misfits of the toy world, comes off as rather stern.

None of these adults even attempts to understand Rudolph's difference or Hermey's unusual career choice. Full of bluster and self-centered, they prove both unable and unwilling to see what the next generation has to offer. Rudolph and Hermey have little choice but to leave: there is simply no place for them in Christmastown.

In the end, of course, all of these matters are resolved, but one could argue that a residue remains: the roar of the Bumble, the surliness of Santa, and the bluster of the Elf Foreman continue to echo, even as the credits role. In a latter-day production, one might imagine, these sharper edges would be filed down. But these contrasts—the pathos and bullying, the friendships and parental rejection— become *the* necessary dramatic ingredients. As Rudolph, Hermey, and the gang venture far from home, suffer great hardships, and finally return to reconcile, we travel and suffer with them. This is the genius of Muller's script.

The script is enriched immeasurably by Marks's seven new songs plus one classic, "Rudolph." Personally, the only animated soundtrack that I believe can match *Rudolph the Red-Nosed Reindeer* is the one for *A Charlie Brown Christmas*. Marks, however, worked much closer than did the Vince Guaraldi Trio at matching his lyrics to the qualities of each character. With everything in motion for *Rudolph*, Marks worked on the seven new songs during the winter of 1963–64.

The songs proved a snug fit for both the script and the characters. "We're a Couple of Misfits" solidified Hermey and Rudolph's personalities and friendship, while the hope of "There's Always Tomorrow" resonates from Clarice's deeper understanding of Rudolph. "The Most Wonderful Day of the Year" captures both the faith and despair of being a misfit toy. These songs, enclosed within Muller's humanistic script, proved icing on the Animagic cake. If there is a misfire in the bunch, which is perhaps even heretical to suggest, it was in allowing Sam the Snowman to perform "Silver and Gold" when it better defined Yukon Cornelius's character (before Burl Ives joined the production, Larry D. Mann had been slated to sing it for Yukon).

Rudolph the Red-Nosed Reindeer: Yukon Cornelius, Rudolph, and Hermey (Rankin/ Bass, 1964) | Classic Media

Rudolph the Red-Nosed Reindeer: Burl Ives as Sam the Snowman, with Rudolph (Rankin/Bass, 1964) | NBC/Photofest

One intriguing question is *why* the special even had songs: the animated Christmas special had barely been established in 1963–64, and there was no reason these specials had to rely on music. In fact, most theatrical cartoons were not musicals. It is possible that Rankin/Bass and GE simply needed Marks's cooperation, which meant bringing the songwriter on board the project as a cocreator. Another influence may have been *Mister Magoo's Christmas Carol*, the first animated Christmas special, in 1962. GE had missed an opportunity to sponsor *Magoo's Christmas Carol*, and *Rudolph* was partially the company's attempt to correct an earlier mistake. And it would be difficult for everyone involved with *Rudolph* to be unaware that *Magoo's Christmas Carol* was a musical, written by Jule Styne and Bob Merrill. Whatever the inspiration or reason, Marks succeeded by writing down-to-earth songs that perfectly harmonized with *Rudolph*'s characters.

GE Presents—*Rudolph the Red-Nosed Reindeer*

Like all things Rudolph, the television show was a commercial venture. Rankin/ Bass was funded by GE and the program broadcast on NBC, a three-year arrangement that proved beneficial—meaning profitable—to everyone involved. It is unclear how permission was gained to use Rudolph's image, but Johnny Marks's involvement (he lived in a brownstone next to Rankin in New York City) probably gave the project the green light. Whether Robert L. May was involved remains an open question. The commercial venture, however, focused on the basics. There was no merchandising of dolls or products. Instead, GE used the characters from *Rudolph* on television and in print advertisements to sell the company's small appliances for the home. The success of the program also guaranteed Rankin/ Bass GE funding for future TV specials.

In a contemporary review of *Rudolph,* Harvey Pack joked about the GE tie-in: "Contractual difficulties prevented any record company from issuing an original cast album this year, but if the *show* is as successful as GE and NBC expect, you'll probably be able to get one next Christmas tucked inside your toaster or electric knife. However, if you're desperate for an album right now simply send in the labels from 2,000 price-fixed GE appliances and they'll mail you Johnny Marks and his piano for your Christmas pleasure."[4] *Rudolph* was meant to entertain *and* sell products.

One intriguing twist in the creation of Rankin/Bass's *Rudolph* was the role of GE vice president Willard H. Sahloff. Some twenty-five years earlier, Sahloff had been an executive at Montgomery Ward, where "at Sahloff's urging" Robert May "developed the little deer into a full-blown promotional character." This was after May had received the copyright for Rudolph in 1947. Sahloff also told May that Rudolph "could be merchandised."[5] Now at GE, Sahloff revived his interest in Rudolph: "Two years ago, when considering a special program for an annual Christmas season activity on the new *General Electric Fantasy Hour,* Sahloff recalled Rudolph, the little red nosed reindeer he had watched, and at least partly inspired, on its climb to fame many years ago in Chicago."[6] Sahloff took the Rudolph idea to ad manager M. M. Masterpool and the Maxon advertising agency (GE's ad agency at the time). Maxon put the wheels for the program in motion.

In 1962, Rankin and Bass had completed the animated *Return to Oz*, an hour television special that followed the plot of the original *Wizard of Oz*. W. W. Lewis, who worked as Maxon's television production supervisor, contacted Arthur Rankin and Jules Bass because "'Return to Oz' had excited the agency and later the audiences that saw the production. . . . Rankin, Bass and Lewis collectively blueprinted the hour-long musical story of Rudolph to be produced with Videocraft's 'Animagic' technique and secured television and motion picture rights."[7] Maxon would shape other key elements of *Rudolph*: "As the hour-long feature began to take shape, the creative group at Maxon felt that greater impact could be achieved if the commercials were integrated into the program by using some of the show's animated characters to deliver the product message. Santa's elves drew the assignment and will sing the praises of the sponsor's products. The feature film's Animagic techniques are to be used in presenting the characters delivering the commercials on sets similar to those in the feature."[8] Three two-minute commercials, including "special music and lyrics extolling the virtues of four General Electric appliances," would be synchronized with the program. *Rudolph*, created and overseen by Videocraft and Maxon, would offer a unified vision of art and commerce.[9]

The idea of Videocraft producing commercials for Maxon and GE may seem unusual today, but the company—in business since 1955—also specialized in commercial work. "The company's commercial division produces for most of the agencies in town. They were 'Clio' winners at the recent 1964 American Tv Commercials Festival for the best in home appliances."[10] With this experience, it would have been surprising if Maxon and GE had asked any other company to produce the commercials.

These holiday specials had perhaps one drawback: they had no regular television time slot. That meant that room would have to be made for *Rudolph* by temporarily bumping other programs off the air. In this case, *Rudolph* replaced *The General Electric College Bowl* and *Meet the Press*, in the 5:30-to-6:30 p.m. slots.

To top everything off, Maxton and GE planned to "juice up the promotion" of *Rudolph*, guaranteeing a large audience share. With *Return to Oz*, ads had run in Sunday papers and TV *Guide*, and a promo was aired on *General Electric College Bowl*. All these promotions, "leading up to the show date, likely aided the Nielsen credit of a 23.5 rating with an almost 42 percent share of the viewing audience." The article continues, "Similar promotion for the early December showing of Rudolph is planned with the campaign slated to start in early fall." The elf advertisements "will also be shown on the *General Electric College Bowl* . . . during the Christmas selling season, which will introduce Rudolph's elves to television a few weeks before the second *Fantasy Hour*."[11] *Rudolph*, thanks to the coffers of GE, would be afforded every opportunity to shine for a large audience.

And exactly how many people did they believe would watch *Rudolph*? According to a *Billboard* piece about Marks and "Rudolph" (the song), the projection for viewers was forty million. *Billboard* offered the sunniest of scenarios for the young buck's future: "'Rudolph' keeps on growing in popularity, and is getting more and more exposure."[12]

Television seems to have found its Christmas niche with *Rudolph*. Most of the classic Christmas songs had been written by 1964, and there had been no classic holiday movies after *White Christmas* in 1954. While television had proven a larger draw than the movies or radio during the 1950s, Christmas on television seemed less distinct. With the changing fortunes of the American family and the stagnation of all things Christmas in the mid-1960s, television offered the potential for a new kind of holiday tradition capable of reflecting these changes. Yearly Christmas specials, both new and as reruns, filled that role during the 1960s and 1970s.

This niche for holiday specials also seemed marked by a changing popular culture. American teens could now listen to the Beatles and the Rolling Stones, while their little brothers and sisters, in the company of Mom and Dad, could watch *Rudolph* and *A Charlie Brown Christmas*. The teen rock culture mostly ignored Christmas, viewing it as unable to carry the serious themes of generational conflict and social rebellion. As a result, Rankin/Bass worried less about selling Christmas to everyone—as Bing Crosby and Gene Autry had done with the "Rudolph" recording—and focused on the family audience. Made for kids and paid for by adult purchases, *Rudolph* and the Christmas shows that followed worked within a narrower cultural field. It may have been a niche, but it was an extremely popular and profitable one.

GE and other advertisers had also learned how to exploit the *Rudolph* franchise more directly. In 1939 Montgomery Ward gave away *Rudolph* books to children accompanied by adults. Later, a line of Rudolph products sold by Ward's made the connection between the story and advertising stronger. Through the medium of TV, however, GE had immediate access to a much larger audience than Montgomery Ward could have imagined. The dual use of the elves in the *Rudolph* program and GE commercials helped blur the lines between commerce and entertainment. Rudolph's fame and the show's popularity could be tied to toaster ovens, automatic knives, and waffle irons for Christmas. Expressed cynically, GE used a children's story to reach adult wallets.

One other aspect of GE's control of *Rudolph*'s purse strings bears comment. In 1965 decisions were made to alter the content of the original program. GE decided that the "Misfits" sequence should be replaced with a new song sequence, "Fame and Fortune." Also, Rankin/Bass responded to viewer criticism that Santa Claus never physically returned to the Island of Misfit Toys. These changes, ready for the 1965 viewing, would constitute the official Rankin/Bass *Rudolph* for over thirty years. Furthermore, demand for commercial space led to certain sequences being cut from the program. For those watching *Rudolph* in 1964, they viewed a program that would never be shown again. For those (like myself) coming to the program later, they would never view the original. Even now, after much of the footage has been restored, the original ending has disappeared. Whatever the claim critics make for Rankin/Bass's *Rudolph* as quality programming, the ultimate control of the program's content rested with GE.

Rudolph Goes Down in TV History

As with the familiar *Rudolph* story line, it is easy to forget that the animation of this Rankin/Bass special was rather simple because it was cheaply made for television. United Productions of America (UPA) and others had created a new, more basic style of animation, and Rankin/Bass drew from available techniques based on a modest budget. The Animagic technique that Rankin/Bass used was the "name for a method of producing dimensional stop-motion photography, i.e., three-dimensional objects and puppets which move on the screen without strings or hands."[13] An animation team in Japan, Dentsu Co., primarily used eight-to-ten-inch, adjustable puppets (the Abominable Snowman had to be scaled much larger), allowing each character to be moved into position and then captured on 35 mm film. This detailed work, naturally, required patience, "and as many as a dozen technicians standing in the wings, waiting for their cues to 'act' their puppets according to the director's instructions."[14] While economics may have dictated the method of *Rudolph*, the Animagic technique helped Rankin/Bass craft their own visual style.

While baby boomers who grew up with Rankin/Bass probably accepted the stop-motion technique without questioning its aesthetics, those raised on Warner or Disney cartoons from the 1940s and 1950s probably viewed it as cheap. Whether artistic or just doing the best it could, though, *Rudolph*'s quirky style meshes well with the idiosyncratic world that these stop-motion characters inhabit.

And an idiosyncratic world it is. *Rudolph* retains an air of the surreal, with a talking snowman, misfit toys, and an angry Santa; more than Andersen's ugly duckling, we have the sharp edges of the Brothers Grimm. The herky-jerky movements and speech of the puppets themselves, even in retrospect, have an air of the unreal. The *Fantasy Hour* lived up to its billing, creating a strange, other-world cobbled together from Santa lore (the elves), folk myths (the abominable snowman), and Alaskan gold mining history (a prospector). A bird that swims, a water pistol that shoots jelly, and a boat that sinks—all add another layer of strangeness.

Rudolph the Red-Nosed Reindeer: Santa and Rudolph (Rankin/Bass, 1964) | NBC/Photofest

The joyous world of Christmastown and the wild North evoked both children's fantasies and nightmares.

Over time, the Rankin/Bass *Rudolph* would become more familiar, allowing us to bring our own politics and views into the mix. Because it is impossible to turn back the clock and see *Rudolph* as viewers saw the program in 1964, it is easy to interpret *Rudolph* in ways that may have never been intended. Was *Rudolph*'s concern with prejudice a mirror of the civil rights movement? Do the overbearing male figures in *Rudolph* serve, like Betty Freidan's *The Feminine Mystique* (1963), as a patriarchal critique? Any cultural misfit, it seems, could adapt Rudolph's story as his or her own.

While there are probably limits to this kind of interpretation, Rankin/Bass's *Rudolph* segues well with the generational change: 1964 would be the last year of the baby boomers. And the generational conflict within the show can easily be viewed against the backdrop of the tumultuous changes of the 1960s. Debuting a year after Kennedy's assassination, *Rudolph* displayed the same generational disruptions that defined the counterculture during that era. Interpreted in this fashion, Rudolph, Hermey, and others reject the conservative views of those in charge (Santa, parents, the Elf Foreman) and strike out on their own. Reconciliation is possible only when tradition begins to make a place for new ways of thinking.

Still, seeing Rudolph and Hermey as Neal Cassady and Jack Kerouac on a journey to see Ken Kesey may be a stretch. Our heroes are rebels with a righteous cause, only temporarily in conflict with Christmastown. Nonetheless, part of the appeal was the show's willingness to mirror changes in the American family during the early 1960s. Rudolph and Hermey may not want a revolution, but they are far from the compliant, easygoing characters of May's original book in 1939.

Another popular interpretation of *Rudolph* focuses on prejudice or, to borrow a more popular catchword of today, bullying. With a heavy emphasis on problems associated with bullying, Rudolph has been welcomed—once again—into schools. May's original story garnered a short piece of commentary in *Life* in 1950 about prejudice ("Rudolph and the Stinkers"). In the Rankin/Bass special, discrimination is given an even wider treatment. Rudolph is criticized for his nose and Hermey for his career choice, while the characters on the Island of Misfit Toys are unloved because they are different. Even the Bumble seems misunderstood. Over the span of the show, however, the viewer learns a lesson: all of these characters have something to contribute, and all are lovable. *Rudolph*, according to this interpretation, is a lesson *against* bullying.

While well intended, this emphasis overlooks a central theme in Rankin/Bass's *Rudolph*: the main problem for Rudolph and his friends is adults, not children. Yes, the other children (save Clarice) shun Rudolph, *after* Comet has already kicked him out of the Reindeer Games; and the other elves make fun of Hermey,

Rudolph the Red-Nosed Reindeer Soundtrack, audio CD reissue | Classic Media / Photofest

after the Elf Foreman has ridiculed him. Over and over, it is the adults (and specifically, adult males) in *Rudolph* who show bad judgment. Donner bullies Rudolph, making him wear a false nose, while the Elf Foreman even bullies the elves that like to make toys because of a subpar performance during song practice ("We Are Santa's Elves"). Peer bullying is not really a problem in Christmastown. The adults, the authority figures, are the problem.

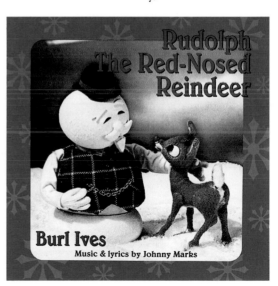

A more obvious truth of Rankin/Bass's *Rudolph* is that adults (again, male adults) are often wrong. They insist that children follow in their footsteps and, when children and wives suggest otherwise, refuse to listen. All these adults seem to carry a pre–World War II idea of the father as the unquestioned head of the household. By failing to understand that the world has changed, they alienate loved ones and place them in harm's way. It is only after the children have left home that the adults see the error of old-think, and even then, the adults come to these revelations only when it is beneficial for them to do so. Luckily for the adults, Hermey and Rudolph return without grudges to take their place within the community.

Instead of cuddly toys for tie-ins, Rankin/Bass have veered closer to the nightmarish world of backwoods folktales. And for most of the show, these nightmares—angry adults, a snow monster, and an Island of Misfit Toys—are as real to a child's worldview as the Wicked Witch of the West in *The Wizard of Oz*. Everyone smiles when Rudolph takes his place at the head of Santa's reindeer team, but when it is time for bed and the lights go out, the giants and misfits return.

This, I believe, is one reason why *Rudolph* has remained so popular. The unkind adults give the show more of an edge than we might expect from family entertainment. One might question whether the people footing the bill for Rudolph (GE) really understood the sharp edges and emotional tumult carried within the stop-motion cartoon. Beneath the shallow veneer of clumsy elves and banjo-playing snowmen, Rankin/Bass embedded a few dark corners into this modern American fairy tale. The characters in *Rudolph* are allowed to make real mistakes, and the children—when all is said and done—are *right*. While everything is smoothed over when the credits roll, including the delivery of the misfit toys, a residue remains: adults are far from infallible. For the young children who watch *Rudolph*, this remains a powerful message.

ten

AN AMERICAN HERO

In the closing pages of this book, it would be tempting to do little more than sing Rudolph's praises. I would argue that praise, at this point, is redundant: any author committed to a book about Rudolph has already sung his praises. While there are many other parts of Rudolph's life that could still be covered (more cartoons, more comics, etc.), it might be more productive and fun to weigh in on Rudolph as a cultural phenomenon—specifically, an American cultural phenomenon that has spread through much of the world. Rudolph, as an ingrained Christmas tradition, as a symbol of heroism, and as a vital piece of commercial folklore, is worth contemplating. What follows, then, is more a meditation on the themes that have run through the book than a summary.

One thing that puzzled me—before I even started this book—was why no one else had already written it. Rudolph seems to qualify as one of those easy, pop-cultural icons like Mickey Mouse and Curious George that invites wide commentary. Every fall, dozens of new books about Santa Claus flood the market, from newly illustrated copies of Clement C. Moore's "A Visit from St. Nicholas" to academic treatments revolving around sacred mushroom cults. As part of Santa's entourage, Rudolph might expect a little bit of the adoration to spill over, but no such luck.

My original answer rested on common sense. Rudolph's story inspired hundreds of articles, but most of what there was to say—about May, Marks, Autry, and Rankin/Bass—could be said in an article. And it also seemed that whatever there was to be said had *already* been said, many times. With the exception of Autry, the bios of Rudolph's creators seemed meager and fairly straightforward. May, for instance, spent much of his life working for Ward's. Indeed, for May and Marks, Rudolph *was* their biography. Even if I combined all the articles about Rudolph and his creators, there would still be too little for an entire book. Viewed in this way, most journalists and academics viewed Rudolph as unpromising material for a book-length project.

This seeming lack of material was complicated by another problem centered on the reality that was Rudolph: he was a story, with a number of slight variations, for children. As a picture book or novelty song or family cartoon, Rudolph never garnered serious attention. He was kids' stuff. I am not speaking here of Rudolph's real value, only a very old cultural prejudice against children's culture. With all things Rudolph, the surface is *all* there is to see. This prejudice, I believe, kept any journalist from writing a sourced story about May or Marks, and it kept biographers from penning a decent essay about either. When James H. Barnett wrote a serious critique about Rudolph in 1954, even going to the trouble to contact May, it proved the exception: other writers quoted it because it was the *only* critique of Rudolph.

My next answer to why no one had written a book about Rudolph, after poring over May's scrapbook and papers, reading dozens of comic books, and collecting all the Rudolph lore I could get my hands on, rested on a more experienced common sense. Surely there was more than enough material for a book. But when considered from a folklorist's point of view, Rudolph has an image problem. Even today, when we celebrate his seventy-fifth birthday (2015), Rudolph's commercial roots remain a problem. Anthropologists may refer to the American Santa Claus as an invented tradition, but the older Saint Nicholas still left traces. Rudolph, by comparison, had been cut from whole cloth. Reindeer were a traditional part of Christmas only because Clement Moore had included them in "A Visit from St. Nicholas" in 1823. Rudolph's roots can be traced no further than the desk of a

Montgomery Ward copywriter, removing both the romanticism and authenticity of his creation.

These are the reasons, I believe, that Rudolph has been less studied than his reputation deserves. Because he is a commercial creation for children at Christmas, no one has been quite sure how to approach Rudolph. Unfortunately, the fact that very few researchers have followed in Barnett's footsteps means that a great deal of Rudolph lore has disappeared forever. Curiously, even most of the people involved in creating Rudolph books, films, and songs did a very poor job of preserving this lore. Partly, the cynic in me suggests, this was purposeful. Any fuller portrait of Rudolph would be problematic because it would underline the fact that he *has* origins, and a copywriter's, no less.

A fuller portrait of Rudolph nonetheless starts with considering his earlier flights, and I would argue that Rudolph found his true place in American holiday culture in 1946. The Depression was over, the war had ended, and Americans were very optimistic about the future. The nostalgia of "White Christmas" still moved many Americans, but a forward-looking era favored exuberant songs and stories along with an emphasis on youth. In colloquial terms, American families had paid their dues and now it was time to party.

When Robert May and Montgomery Ward took Rudolph out of mothballs for the Christmas of 1946, the lining up of image and an era could not have been more fortuitous. Rudolph's story may have been based on Andersen's "The Ugly Duckling," but the ugly duckling—after transforming into a beautiful swan—never *does* anything. He just enjoys the feeling of being a beautiful swan (and Ferdinand the Bull was even worse, because he did not want to do anything). Rudolph, our modest hero, is a go-getter, ready to do whatever he can when Santa asks for his help. Surely this echoes the American soldier's willingness to do his or her part during the war, but more so, the willingness of the average man or woman to strive toward the American dream (a family, a home, a good job, and a bright future for one's children). More than an ugly duckling, Rudolph was an updated version of the Horatio Alger myth, a folk hero for children who wanted to follow in Dad's footsteps. As many toys prepared kids for adulthood by mirroring the working world (chemistry sets, Lincoln Logs, Erector sets), Rudolph schooled the youngest of the young in the American way of life.

This connects Rudolph (and May, Marks, and Autry) with our favorite myth: American success. The theme runs through all of Rudolph's adventures and is doubled in the portraits of his creators. May in particular made good copy because his trajectory in regard to the American dream echoed Rudolph's story. Earlier inconsistencies in the narrative of Rudolph's origins perhaps resulted from no more than May trying to get the story right. The focus on his first wife dying of cancer was heartrending but too maudlin and too immersed in the Depression era. With a second wife and a growing family, a house in the suburbs, and wealth thanks to Rudolph, May embodied the American success myth of his time. His modesty and gentle humor presented a persona that seemed perfectly in sync with Rudolph.

This idea even connects on a more personal level. It is fairly easy to parallel May's position at Ward's to Rudolph's position at the North Pole: how do I fit in *and* stand out? And undoubtedly many Americans, working for larger corporations after World War II, found themselves in the same position as May. The era of John D. Rockefeller now made way for the era of Dale Carnegie and Norman Vincent Peale. Instead of conquistadores, business needed company men of good character with the right kind of ambition. May and Rudolph qualified and then some.

The American success myth also points to the real difference between *Rudolph* (1939) and *The Story of Ferdinand* (1936). When May's boss asked him to write a story like *Ferdinand*, he probably meant no more than an attractive children's story about a cute animal. Clearly, though, no one wanted a Christmas story about a reindeer who was so laid back he refused to help Santa out when needed (much less one who, in the face of war, became a pacifist). *Ferdinand* struck a chord with Americans, but he never *seemed* very American. *Rudolph*, in fact, would need to be *Ferdinand*'s opposite: an optimistic go-getter who always believed, if he did his best, in a brighter tomorrow. With one eye on Disney's animated shorts like *Ferdinand* in 1938 and *The Ugly Duckling* in 1939, May overlaid a Horatio Alger chassis on Rudolph. Like Disney's main star, Mickey, Rudolph would be 100 percent American.

A fuller portrait of Rudolph also requires filling in the other half of his story: for each of his major growth spurts, a corporation has stood behind Rudolph. Americans seem to be in the habit of seeing individuals—May, Marks, Autry, and Rankin/Bass—instead of the businesses that back them, because we have been trained to see that way. We love the story of the individual, plying his or her art, and eventually—once it reaches a popular and perhaps critical saturation point reaping financial rewards. These stories feed the American success myth, but they misrepresent the process. What would Rudolph mean to us today without Montgomery Ward, Columbia Records, and GE? In truth, we have no idea. But a commonsense guess would conclude that Rudolph's flight would have leveled off much sooner without the backing of the marketing and promotion teams of these companies. For every dollar May, Marks, Autry, and Rankin/Bass made from Rudolph, Ward's, Columbia, and GE made a great deal more.

This is not a polemic for or against big business within a consumer culture. The point is how Ward's, in the traditional account of Rudolph, seems almost like a silent partner; the company helped him take his first steps, but then faded into the background as the young buck took his first flight. When we do learn about the role these companies play, it tends to be in stories emphasizing their benevolence. Ward's returned Rudolph's copyright to May; GE funded Rankin/Bass's vision for *Rudolph*; Character Arts (Rudolph's current promotion team) is a family outfit. These acts of kindness and image enhancements always come with strings: Ward's continued to market Rudolph products into the 1990s; GE viewed *Rudolph* as an hour-long announcement for small household appliances; and Creative Arts has allowed an odd assortment of advertisers to cash in on Rudolph's good name. Even when the stories about May, Marks, and others are truthful, they fill in only one side of a very unbalanced equation.

A fuller portrait also considers that when the wheel turned in the mid-1960s, Rudolph turned with it. With Rankin/Bass, we have a slightly older Rudolph who echoed his earlier persona; he still strove to do his best and to play his part in the larger world of Christmastown. But as the generation gap opened up (seemingly, the gap had hardly existed in 1946), Rudolph, along with his good friend Hermey, proved willing to go his own way. While Rudolph may have been a poor fit for the counterculture, he nonetheless prized many of the same values: above all, one had to be true to oneself. By refusing to stay where they do not fit and are not wanted, Rudolph and Hermey force the older generation (Donner, Comet, Santa Claus, and the Elf Foreman) to make concessions. It is about more than needing Rudolph's red nose on a foggy evening or about needing a dentist at the North Pole. It is about learning to recognize everyone's gift and finding a place within Christmastown to express these gifts. Even the mighty Bumble, we learn toward the story's end, has a place. Cultures must grow and be receptive to change, or else, as in Christmastown, toothaches go untreated and Christmas is canceled. Rudolph remains an American hero, albeit one with a stronger, more singular voice.

In many ways, Rudolph's story comes to an impasse after 1964. Despite several other adventures, on TV, in comic books, and in early readers, the Rankin/Bass *Rudolph* was the last Rudolph in sync with the zeitgeist. Indeed, the next two times Rudolph crossed Rankin/Bass's path leave the impression that the team sleepwalked through the latter half of the 1970s. Both *Rudolph's Shiny New Year's* (1976) and *Rudolph and Frosty's Christmas in July* (1979) are shambolic messes. With their fragmented plots, quirky, unfunny characters, and terrible songs, the viewer is reminded of how simplistic stop-motion can look without the supporting components. What must have seemed like a reboot in 1998, *Rudolph the Red-Nosed Reindeer: The Movie*, fared no better.

After various attempts to revive or profit from new ventures, the various parties who hold Rudolph's trademark came to a singular decision. The 1964 Rudolph, for all intents and purposes, would become the only Rudolph. His story, aired each year, staged, printed in a graphic comic, and depicted on U.S. stamps, remains frozen in an earlier time and place. While both licensing opportunities (ornaments, figurines) and school programs (anti-bullying) argue relevancy, a whiff of nostalgia and feel-good propaganda dilute the claim. The very innocence for which we praise Rankin/Bass's *Rudolph* spells out a mythic dead end: when the object we love evokes no more than the past, we have lost something; when what we love requires a conscious effort to explain its relevancy, we no longer feel it; no longer living folklore, a myth becomes a shadow of its former self.

This seems to be a decision—focusing on the 1964 special—that the franchise owners came to only over time. In 1989, during Rudolph's fiftieth anniversary, May's children (he had died in 1976) pushed Rudolph—the original one—back into the limelight. That year, one-half of the Rudolph franchise (May's half) strived to remind the public of the person who had created him: "Gradually," a *Chicago Tribune* article noted, "the song usurped the book's place in the nation's collective memory."[1] The original book, in fact, had been out of print for some time. In the article, the Rankin/Bass cartoon is barely mentioned. "Now," the *Chicago Tribune* continued, "the May family just hopes Robert May's original Rudolph—and his book—are back for good."[2] Barbara May Lewis, May's first audience for *Rudolph*, seconded these sentiments. "[The success] is fine with me. But I'm somewhat of a purist. I prefer the original story."[3]

The merchandizing at this point (1989) also rested in the May camp. There were no official replicas of Rudolph, Hermey, and the Island of Misfit Toys until 1998, over thirty years after the show had originally aired. Perhaps the fact that May had already been franchising Rudolph created a problem or conflict for Rankin/Bass merchandise back in 1964: May's *Rudolph*, with a copyright dating to 1939, was already on the market. Whatever the complications and conflicts between copyright owners (the Mays and Markses), the Applause merchandising company gave Rudolph a makeover in 1989, but one that in no way resembled the character from the Rankin/Bass show.

But a fundamental shift in all things Ru-

dolph occurred after this much-touted fiftieth anniversary, a change that would be fully realized during a *second* fiftieth anniversary in 2014. This second fiftieth anniversary was brought about by a simple accident of history: Rankin/Bass's *Rudolph* (1964) aired twenty-five years after May's *Rudolph* (1939). In 1989 the original Rudolph turned fifty, leading to a marketing blitz of dolls and trinkets for middle-aged baby boomers. In 2014 the primary focus was on the fiftieth year of the Rankin/Bass *Rudolph*, with the marketing blitz shifting to Rudolph, Hermey, and the Island of Misfit Toys. The owners of Rudolph's trademark, with lots of help from Creative Arts, had reinvented their brand.

This shift was obvious, for instance, when the U.S. Postal Service issued a block of Rudolph stamps in 2014. The USPS block featured Rudolph, Hermey and Rudolph, Santa Claus, and the Bumble. Other post office products would also be offered, including a framed picture of Rudolph with a stamp set insert for $19.95. In dedicating the stamps, Postmaster General Patrick Donahoe said, "Rudolph's story of guiding Santa's sleigh on Christmas Eve has been revered by families for five decades. We're celebrating that milestone by having our fleet of 212,000 'sleighs' deliver Rudolph and his friends on 500 million Forever stamps to nearly 153 million addresses this holiday season."[4] The postal service's lack of awareness that Rudolph had been "revered" for twenty-five years before 1964 seems like a bad case of selective memory. As far as the Postal Service was concerned, May and the earlier Rudolph had never existed.

Why not print a block of four stamps featuring the original illustrations by Denver Gillen, celebrating Rudolph's seventy-fifth birthday? An educated guess would focus on self-promotion, economics, and name recognition for the USPS and Creative Arts. The Rankin/Bass *Rudolph* is seemingly the most recognizable Rudolph; because of this, the Rankin/Bass *Rudolph* is the only Rudolph that the copyright holders wish to exploit; and, with the same logic, the Rankin/Bass *Rudolph* seems to have the most potential for a successful stamp issue. It is a win-win situation for the copyright holders and the USPS: Rudolph wins free exposure, and the USPS sells a lot of postage stamps.

Today, focusing on Rankin/Bass's 1964 special is a perfect business model,

Rudolph the Red-Nosed Reindeer's fiftieth-anniversary stamp issue (USPS, 2014)

Hooves of Fire (1999) | CBS/ Photofest

no doubt, but a very conservative one. It assures that all things Rudolph will be about glancing longingly toward the past, even when creating new works such as a musical based on the Rankin/Bass program. Ironically, just as copyright holders sealed Rudolph's fate to the nostalgia market, other creative souls have reimagined his heroic persona in a contemporary setting. Programs have either exploited the tradition of reindeer at Christmas, skirting Rudolph's copyright by creating a *new* reindeer, or lambasted the Rankin/Bass *Rudolph* with satire and parody. In pushing beyond the family-centered Disney-Rudolph Inc. model, these creators have mined a much richer vein of holiday lore.

The three Robbie Reindeer cartoons push Santa's reindeer into a contemporary setting. These cartoons are cut from a hipper entertainment world, creating cartoons for kids while still encoding the material for adults. The background joke for Robbie, and the aspect of these cartoons that relates directly to the subject at hand, is his parentage: his father is Rudolph. This, however, can never be said for two reasons. First, Robbie is very sensitive about the fact, and second, copyright. The show's makers, in fact, seem to be having fun with the viewer and winking at the copyright holder.

Robbie's first adventure, *Hooves of Fire*, aired in Britain in 1999, a year after the debacle of *Rudolph the Red-Nosed Reindeer: The Movie*. Here we meet our hero, Robbie, a reindeer with a good nose for directions but an underachiever: he would rather eat cheeseburgers and laze around than exercise. His dad (Rudolph), however, has sent him to Coldchester—Santa's northern headquarters—for character building with the rest of the reindeer team. Unfortunately, Blitzen hates Robbie, just like he hated Robbie's father, and works hard to make sure he fails. With the help of female Donner (an eventual love interest) and Old Jingle (a Yoda-like spiritual trainer), Robbie eventually comes into his own. While he loses the reindeer games, Blitzen is disqualified (he seems to be on steroids). For a romantic finale, Santa loans Robbie the new, souped-up sleigh for the night, and he and Donner fly to the moon.

This quick plot outline, however, fails to convey that *Hooves of Fire* is fun stuff, a hip homage to *Rudolph* that never gets bogged down in its reverence. The lovable loser Robbie plops down into a vibrant stop-motion world, surrounded by sharply drawn characters. Santa Claus, known as Weirdy-Beardy, carefully combs his closet for stylish clothing; Old Jingle offers Robbie the sage advice, echoing Yoda from *Star Wars*, "Use the nose jump"; and the real competition takes place at Robbie's lodging, where Prancer, Vixen, Donner, and the others learn to live with the conniving Blitzen.[5] *Hooves of Fire* also pokes fun at Rudolph lore: Robbie's toy creations Sebastian Muscle Whale and OctoMonkey seem destined for the Island of Misfit Toys, while his love interest, the female Donner, was the reindeer who played Rudolph's father in the 1964 *Rudolph*. Indeed, the very concept of the episode, that Robbie *is* Rudolph's son, seems to poke a finger in the eye of the copyright holder.

At the bottom of all this, *Hooves of Fire* excels in the same arena as the Rankin/Bass *Rudolph*: Robbie has lots of heart. Robbie still strives to be a hero, just like his dad, but the world he must thrive in is filled with a more complex set of reindeer games. His success comes less from his natural-born talent—a nose that can find any spot on the globe—than from his willingness to dig deep within his own character to find the true Robbie.

If Robbie seemed like a buoyant step in the right direction, Corky Quakenbush's *Rudolph* parodies must have seemed—to some—like one step over the line. In three four-minute segments, *Raging Rudolph*, *The Reinfather*, and *A Pack of Gifts Now*, Quakenbush combines Rankin/Bass with Martin Scorsese to create violent and very funny homages/parodies to Rankin/Bass's *Rudolph*.

Quakenbush's first parody, *Raging Rudolph*, most closely resembles—in its portrayal of Christmastown, Rudolph and Hermey's relationship, and a grumpy Santa Claus—the original Rankin/Bass show. The program is billed as a "Martin Scorsese and Rankin/Bass Picture," and as it opens, we meet an Italian-accented Snowman, seated at a table eating scungilli ("Hey, what's so freakin' important you interrupted my scungilli?").[6] The Snowman tells how Rudolph always wanted to "be one of Santa's made reindeer." When two other young reindeer see his nose (Frankie Two Times and Jimmy the Antler), one holds him while the other kicks the crap out of him. Now in a neck brace ("I guess I'm just a —— misfit"), Rudolph meets Hermey the Drill, whom Santa has kicked out for refusing to pay tribute.[7] The two misfits sing a rousing version of "We'll Get Even" and together call on hit man Yukon Corleone to take Santa out.

The scene switches to Santa's workshop, where an elf carries a bagful of money, and the head man reports that "Donner and Blitzen just hijacked a shipment of pure snow." Yukon, however, breaks up the party (Santa asks, "Who the —— are you?"). Yukon opens fire, taking out Santa and the elves. He places the head of the last elf in a vise and tightens it until the elf's head explodes. Back at the elf shop, another reindeer continues to make fun of Rudolph (calling him "fireplug") until Hermey opens a box with Santa's head in it. The Bumble (an enforcer) takes Santa's head and sticks it on top of the Christmas tree. Rudolph becomes the capo, with Hermey as his lieutenant, and the Snowman delivers the final message: "So remember kids, the moral of this story is keep your —— mouth shut!"[8]

For those who believe in the innocence to Rankin/Bass's *Rudolph*, this is sacrilege; for boomers who watched *Rudolph* in childhood (1960s) and came of age with American cinema in the 1970s, it is pure genius. Quakenbush deconstructs the program, in the old-fashioned sense of the word; the cute elves and reindeer of Christmastown become inner-city mobsters bent on revenge. *Rudolph*, 1964, is turned on his head. Even so, for those who get them, these short parodies are also a celebration of the stop-motion holiday specials from that period. To appreciate these parodies, the audience has to understand that a director only goes to the trouble to lambaste something he loves; taking *Rudolph* apart allows the accepting viewer to put him back together for a new era.

At the end of 2001, *Saturday Night Live* followed with its own replay of Rankin/Bass's *Rudolph*, juxtaposing the innocence of the original with a post-9/11 world. While most satire seems satisfied to make people laugh, "The Narrator That Ruined Christmas" seems to pose an unanswerable question: What is the value of *Rudolph*, or any holiday entertainment, when measured against the daily news headlines?

"The Narrator That Ruined Christmas" opens with Sam the Snowman playing his familiar role, beginning the story of Rudolph, the Bumble, and the Christmas that was almost canceled. He soon breaks his own narration, however, along with the fourth wall: "I'm sorry. It just all seems so trivial right now. I mean, we're still in Afghanistan, this country's under siege . . . we're getting warnings every week. And what are we talking about here, an abominable snow monster? Ooh, a snow monster, I'm so scared! Let's all worry about some crappy-ass snow monster. Come on, folks, you watch CNN. I'm holding three months of Cipro up my butt hole and I'm supposed to pick up a freakin' banjo and sing? Screw it, I can't do this." Instead of continuing as he has in the past, the Snowman walks away. In the next scene, a little boy and girl stare at the scenery of *Rudolph* without the narrator. When they question his absence, he momentarily returns. "Don't you get it?" the Snowman angrily asks. "It's not important anymore."[9]

Next, we see Sam the Snowman at home in an unkempt igloo, snoozing (the television news has been left on). The boy and girl continue to speak to Sam by way of the television, asking about the misfit toys. As he sarcastically mimics the children (sounding a little bit like a grown-up version of Cartman from *South Park*), Rudolph and Hermey drop by and ask him to reconsider. Sam remains adamant: "This Christmas we're gonna do something that matters—meet us downtown." Briefly, Mr. and Mrs. Claus complain about the turn of events, asking where Sam has gone with the children. At the next scene, Sam, Rudolph, Hermey, and the children stand behind a "Do Not Cross" blockade, with Rudolph saying, "I don't like Ground Zero."[10] Rudolph becomes a blood donor (with the needle injected directly into his nose), while Sam tries to get through the police line to build the morale of the cleanup effort. The police hold Sam back but allow Jerry Stiller inside the barricade: Sam keeps getting angrier.

Finally, Santa arrives on the scene, speaking to Sam and delivering what seems like the true moral of this short parody: "It's not about you, douche bag. No one needs your self-important grandstanding. Don't you see? You show-biz types are just trying to shift the focus away from the crisis and onto yourselves. You're an entertainer. It's a simple job, OK, do a dance, show us your boobs, and make us happy, monkey." Santa's speech is combined with a children's song inciting

Sam (and all entertainers) to "paint your ass red, and shake, shake, shake it."[11] This convinces Sam, who restarts his narration, only to be interrupted by an NBC Special Report. Following the report asking citizens to "panic and not to enjoy themselves" for the next forty-five minutes, Sam breaks his banjo over his head.[12]

Exactly what a viewer might make of all this—outside of comic relief—will vary greatly. The message at first seems to hark back to *Sullivan's Travels* (1941), with the falling action suggesting that entertainment—in the midst of hard times—is really what the people need. But even those unschooled in Frankfurt ideology could note that entertainment is a good way to distract the people from the politics or crisis of the moment. With "The Narrator That Ruined Christmas," I believe we are left with two points. One, that instead of making a meaningful gesture, Sam, in his grandstanding, draws attention to himself. Still, Sam is partly right. The world of *Rudolph* circa 1964 seems trivial when forced to compete for air time with current events. We may love *Rudolph*, but in a post-9/11 world, it becomes harder and harder to return to this more innocent time.

While these short parodies will never capture the audience that Rankin/Bass's *Rudolph* did, and while they will probably never become yearly family traditions, they are vital commentaries on our love affair with the original and Rudolph's place in the contemporary world. It is ironic that satire has the power—legally—to evade the copyright holders, because these works have the ability to undermine the myth of the original. They are also one of the few places in which the folklore of Rudolph seems to be alive. These satires are born of childhood dreams but leavened with adult realities: the world of Rankin/Bass is a wonderful place to visit, but no longer one—in the post-9/11, world—that anyone could or should fully embrace.

It is also interesting to juxtapose these parodies with recent Rudolph commercials, the one arena in which the copyright holders have allowed him to appear in new narratives. In 2007 Rudolph the Red-Nosed Reindeer and a number of his friends appeared in a thirty-second spot for Aflac Insurance. Rudolph is in bed with a cold (he is sneezing) and worried: "I hope I don't miss work this Christmas."[13] He is surrounded by characters from the Rankin/Bass special. Clarice seems equally worried: "Yeah, how will you pay for things like food, electricity . . ." and, from Hermey, "dental bills." Yukon offers: "Gadzooks! You need a backup plan!" Luckily, Santa arrives informing everyone that there is nothing to worry about: "Ho-ho-ho! That's why we have Aflac." Rudolph chimes back in, "So I'll have cash to help pay the bills."[14] There is still a problem, however: What if Rudolph is still not better by Christmas? No worries: the Aflac duck will take his place.

Who is this advertisement aimed at? Probably aging baby boomers who grew up with Rankin/Bass's *Rudolph*. In other words, nostalgia for *Rudolph* works to gather viewers' attention, leading them to wonder if they are underinsured. Bob Garfield expanded on this in *Ad Age*: "Of course it will resonate with Mom and Dad. The idea of facing the holidays with reduced wages is one of the top parental nightmares. And because every single nonimmigrant American worker or employer with school-age kids has lived with the Rudolph cartoon for a lifetime, it is, on the face of it, an ideal vehicle for getting attention."[15] The magic of Rankin/Bass's *Rudolph*, then, is now supposed to frighten boomers into purchasing insurance.

A Verizon spot featuring the Island of Misfit Toys is equally problematic. When a cell phone arrives on the island, the Spotted Elephant asks: "What are you doing here?"[16] In fact, the misfit toys seem puzzled until the message "AT&T 3G Coverage" pops up: "Ohhhh." This phone with its poor coverage really is a misfit, leading the airplane toy to say, "You're gonna fit right in here."[17] Here we have moved from inciting fear to sell insurance to making fun of a cell phone with poor coverage (and who knows whether the claim is even true). Both commercials turn the original Rankin/Bass message inside out. The Aflac spot clearly qualifies as a downgrading of Rudolph as commercial folklore: instead of representing the dreams of children, Rudolph has become an adult with adult responsibilities. This would be a sad way for Rudolph the Red-Nosed Reindeer to be remembered.

In his 1979 book, *Yearning for Yesterday*, Fred Davis ends with several observations about "contemporary nostalgia" that speak to commercial folk creations like Rudolph. "Perhaps the first and most obvious thing to note about contemporary nostalgia," he begins, "is that it is very big business."[18] Davis even argues that history, as in Disney's replica of "American small-town life circa 1900,"

> is dwarfed by the near worshipful attention lavished on the characters, plots, scenes, and events from Walt Disney's own animated cartoons and feature films. And this, perhaps, is a clue to what is most striking and interesting about contemporary nostalgia, namely, that not only is it propagated on a vast scale by the mass media but the very objects of collective nostalgia are in themselves media creations from the recent past. In other words, in their ceaseless search for new marketable objects of nostalgia the media now do little but devour themselves. Or, as a cynic might put it, nostalgia exists of the media, by the media, and for the media.[19]

Instead of speaking of family holiday traditions drawn from ethnic or regional heritage, as Laura Ingalls Wilder did in her *Little House* books, we now collectively remember the Coca-Cola Santa and Montgomery Ward's Rudolph.

Because Rudolph and the Coca-Cola Santa have identifiable origins, however, these origins are problematic to those who promote their images. As with playing down Rudolph's business roots, obscuring his origins leaves the impression of real folklore in a misty past: "Because there is money to [be] made from nostalgia the media have come to devour their past creations at an ever increasing rate. A consequence has been that the time span between the 'original appearance,' as it were, and its nostalgic recycling has shrunk to a fraction of what it once was. Oddly, the recent past is made to seem as a result more removed and historic than previous ways of subjectively relating to it would have made it appear."[20] Instead of seeming like a book, song, or cartoon created in a specific place and time, Rudolph takes on the aura of an embedded tradition. In this way, myth and nostalgia work together to erase historical origins and markings. In the process, Rudolph, like Mickey, Donald, and Bugs Bunny, becomes ahistorical.

Nostalgia has been a particularly powerful drug for baby boomers, and per-haps—as we grow older—the drug of choice. Fred Davis and others have argued that the disruptions of the 1960s—President Kennedy's assassination (1963), Vietnam, and both Martin Luther King Jr. and Robert Kennedy's assassinations (1968)—caused baby boomers to seek a time and place before adolescence. In movies and TV the 1950s (*Happy Days*) and very early 1960s (*American Graffiti*) became that time and place. The nature of Rankin/Bass's *Rudolph*—a fantasy animated cartoon for children—makes it easy for aging boomers to embrace it as a marker from a more innocent time. Naturally, non–baby boomers also experience nostalgia, and Christmas remains the most nostalgic holiday of all. But many boomers, coming of age during the 1950s and early 1960s, have a special relationship with Rudolph. In memory and merchandising, the relationship remains a strong one.

Rudolph has now taken his place beside Santa as an indispensable part of an American Christmas, but he deserves more than to be relegated to the status of nostalgia. The original sources of our Rudolph favorites—the 1939 book, the 1949 song, and 1964 cartoon—remain dynamic legacies. And like preindustrial folklore, reading the book, singing the song, and watching the cartoon serve as rituals for millions of families every holiday season. Since his inception, though, the power of Rudolph's myth—the very longevity of it—required an ability to grow and adapt. From Depression-era resilience to a postwar hero for baby boomers, from the first and perhaps only addition to the Santa myth in America to his willingness to question the myth itself, Rudolph's vitality and relevance have been inseparable from his ability to evolve with the times. The question is less whether Rudolph will remain beloved by millions of children and adults in the twenty-first century: clearly he will be. The question is whether Rudolph will be corralled for the gazing pleasure of aging baby boomers or allowed to roam free.

notes

ONE Robert L. May, Montgomery Ward, and a Reindeer Named Rudolph

1. Robert L. May, "Rudolph and I Were Something Alike," *Guideposts*, January 1975, 12.

2. Nate Bloom, "Shining a Light on the Largely Untold Story of the Origins of Rudolph, the Red-Nosed Reindeer," *Interfaith Family*, December 20, 2011, www.interfaithfamily.com.

3. May, "Rudolph and I," 12.

4. Eileen Ogintz, "Afterglow: The Man Who Created Rudolph from an Idea That Almost Didn't Fly," *Chicago Tribune*, December 13, 1990, C19.

5. Jessica Pupovac, "Writing 'Rudolph': The Original Red-Nosed Manuscript," National Public Radio, December 25, 2013, www.npr.org.

6. Priscilla Eliades to Christopher N. May, December 14, 1978, Papers of Robert L. May, Rauner Special Collections Library, Dartmouth College, Hanover, NH (hereafter cited as May Papers).

7. Robert Lewis May, Dartmouth Alumni Questionnaire, November 15, 1960, May Papers.

8. [DeWolfe?], "May Interview," December 7, 1939, May Papers.

9. *Dartmouth Alumni Magazine*, April 1935, 52–53.

10. Ibid., February 1936, 59.

11. May, "Rudolph and I," 12.

12. [DeWolfe?], "May Interview."

13. Eugene Field Society, Honorary Membership, April 19, 1941, May Papers.

14. "'Jingle Bells' Dispute Jangles On," *Washington Times*, December 24, 2003, www.washingtontimes.com.

15. Stanley Frankel to Oscar Dystel at *Coronet*, October 23, 1947, Stanley Frankel Papers, Northwestern University Library.

16. Robert L. May to Charles E. Widmayer, August 27, 1948, May Papers.

17. Ralph H. Major Jr. and Stanley Frankel, "Rudolph That Amazing Reindeer," *Coronet*, December 1948, 147.

18. Ibid.

19. Ibid.

20. Ibid.

21. Ibid., 149.

22. Ibid., 150.

23. Ace Collins, *Stories behind the Best-Loved Songs of Christmas* (Grand Rapids, MI: Zondervan, 2001), 148.

24. Robert L. May, "How Rudolph Came to Christmas," *Spartanburg (SC) Herald-Journal*, December 22, 1963, Family Weekly, 6–7.

25. Ibid.

26. Ibid.

27. Jim Liston, "Rudolph the Red-Nosed Reindeer Took Him for a Ride," *Today's Health*, December 1959, 33.

28. "Rudolph Was Almost Rollo," *Newsweek*, December 7, 1964, 80.

29. May, "Rudolph and I," 13.

30. Ibid.

31. Inez Whiteley Foster, "Red-Nosed Reindeer: Rudolph Finds Way to Little People's Hearts through Robert May," *Christian Science Monitor*, December 4, 1948, 10.

32. Ibid.

33. May, "Rudolph and I," 13.

34. Pupovac, "Writing 'Rudolph.'"

35. Michael Washburn, "Boca Once Was Home to Rudolph's Creator," *Boca Raton (FL) News*, December 14, 1990, 1B.

36. May, "How Rudolph Came to Christmas," 7.

37. May, "Rudolph and I," 15.

38. May, "How Rudolph Came to Christmas," 7.

39. Billy Hallowell, "Do You Know the Real History of 'Rudolph the Red-Nosed Reindeer'?" *Blaze*, December 24, 2011, www.theblaze.com.

40. Bloom, "Shining a Light."

41. Ibid.

TWO Rudolph's First Flight

1. Tim Hollis, *Christmas Wishes: A Catalog of Vintage Holiday Treats and Treasures* (Mechanicsburg, PA: Stackpole Books, 2010), 37.

2. Robert L. May, *Rudolph the Red-Nosed Reindeer* (Carlisle, MA: Applewood, reprint, 1990).

3. Clement C. Moore, "A Visit from St. Nicholas," 1823; Martin Gardner, *The Annotated "Night before Christmas"* (New York: Simon and Schuster, 1991), 39.

4. Tilly Smith, *The Real Rudolph: A Natural History of the Reindeer* (Gloucestershire, UK: Sutton, 2006), 10.

5. Montgomery Ward, "Get Ready for Rudolph the Red-Nosed Reindeer," 1939, May Papers.

6. Ibid.

7. Gary Cross, *An All-Consuming Century: Why Commercialism Won in Modern America* (New York: Columbia University Press, 2000), 68.

8. Steven Mintz and Susan Kellogg, *Domestic Revolutions: A Social History of American Family Life* (New York: Free Press, 1987), 135.

9. Montgomery Ward, *Business Builder*, December 1, 1939, May Papers.

10. Montgomery Ward, "Retail Sales Memo," September 1, 1939, May Papers.

11. Montgomery Ward, "Get Ready for Rudolph."

12. Ibid.

13. Montgomery Ward, *Business Builder*.

14. Montgomery Ward, "Retail Sales Memo."

15. Ibid.

16. Montgomery Ward, "Get Ready for Rudolph."

17. Montgomery Ward, "A Message from Rudolph," December 1939, Montgomery Ward Collection, American Heritage Center, University of Wyoming (hereafter cited as Ward Collection).

18. Ibid.

19. Ibid.

20. Gary Cross, *Kids' Stuff: Toys and the Changing World of American Childhood* (Cambridge, MA: Harvard University Press, 1997), 106.

21. "The Psychology of Toys," *Business Builder*, Montgomery Ward, December 1, 1939, May Papers.

22. Ibid.

23. Ibid.

24. Ibid.

25. John A. Martin, "It's a Gift . . . and a Story!," Montgomery Ward, December 6, 1939, May Papers.

26. "Store Manager Memo," Montgomery Ward, October 27, 1939, May Papers.

27. *Arizona Daily Star*, December 17, 1939.

28. Jack Story to Montgomery Ward, circa 1939, May Papers.

29. George Smith to Robert L. May, November 13, 1939, May Papers.

30. M. Herbert Baker to Robert May, July 5, 1940, May Papers.

31. Sidney Hayward to Robert May, November 16, 1939, May Papers.

32. Raymond Dobson to John Martin, circa 1939, May Papers.

33. Robert L. May to Raymond Dobson, December 19, 1939, May Papers.

34. Sandusky (OH) Newspapers to John Martin, circa 1939, May Papers.

35. Melvin Taylor to John Martin, circa 1939, May Papers.

36. Floyd Edinger to John Martin, circa 1939, May Papers.

37. Ruby Schuyler to the Montgomery Ward Advertising Bureau, November 15, 1939, May Papers.

38. Jennie Waldram to Montgomery Ward, February 24, 1940, May Papers.

39. Susan to Miss Schuyler, December 5, 1939, May Papers.

40. Howard to Miss Schuyler, circa 1939, May Papers.

41. Cross, *Kids' Stuff*, 106.

42. J. Knowles to Retail Advertising Dept., December 28, 1939, May Papers.

43. J. A. Allen to H. E. MacDonald, March 4, 1940, May Papers.

44. Irving Heineman to Robert May, January 26, 1940, May Papers.

45. Ibid.

46. Ibid.

47. Louise Benino to William Simon Jr., January 16, 1940, May Papers.

THREE Rudolph's Second Flight

1. "All Store Managers," Montgomery Ward, March 1, 1940, May Papers.

2. M. O. Boxwell to H. E. MacDonald, August 8, 1940, May Papers.

3. "All Store Managers," Montgomery Ward, March 1, 1940, May Papers.

4. Robert P. Ledermann, *Christmas on State Street: 1940s and Beyond* (Mount Pleasant, SC: Arcadia, 2002), 40.

5. "Benny the Bunny Liked Beans," review, *Kirkus Reviews*, September 16, 1940.

6. Advertisement, *Billboard*, November 6, 1948, 79.

7. Bob May to Dartmouth [Bob], 1946, May Papers.

8. Franklin D. Roosevelt, "Statement on the Seizure of Montgomery Ward Co. Properties," December 27, 1944, www.presidency.ucsb.edu.

9. Cecil C. Hoge Sr., *The First Hundred Years Are the Toughest: What We Can Learn from the Century of Competition between Sears and Wards* (Berkeley, CA: Ten Speed, 1988), 145.

10. Bob May to Dartmouth [Bob], October 19, 1944, May Papers.

11. Ibid.

12. Robert May to Dartmouth [Bob], 1946, May Papers.

13. John A. Martin, December 6, 1946 [this document resembles a press release], May Papers.

14. Ibid.

15. Ibid.

16. "1940 Orders for Give-Away Rudolphs," Montgomery Ward, circa 1940, May Papers.

17. Stan Zielinski, "Rudolph the Red-Nosed Reindeer," *Children's Picturebook Collecting*, November 2, 2008, www.1stedition.net.

18. Ibid.

19. Michael Whorf, *American Popular Song Composers: Oral Histories, 1920s–1950s* (Jefferson, NC: McFarland, 2012), 137.

20. Robert May to Dartmouth [Bob], 1946, May Papers.

21. Cyndi Laurin and Craig Morningstar, *The Rudolph Factor: Finding the Bright Lights That Drive Innovation in Your Business* (Hoboken, NJ: Wiley, 2009), 42.

22. Major and Frankel, "Rudolph That Amazing Reindeer."

23. Tiffany J. Lewis, "Rudolph Goes Down in History," *Premier*, December 1994, 38.

24. Collins, *Stories behind the Best-Loved Songs of Christmas*, 149.

25. Foster, "Red-Nosed Reindeer," 10.

26. May, "Rudolph and I," 15.

27. John A. Martin, "It's a *Gift* . . . and a *Story*!," Montgomery Ward, December 6, 1940, May Papers.

28. Pupovac, "Writing 'Rudolph.'"

FOUR Merchandise and the Baby Boom

1. *Chicago Daily Tribune*, Display ad 101, December 14, 1947, NW3.

2. LeRoy Ashby, *With Amusement for All: A History of American Popular Culture since 1830* (Louisville: University Press of Kentucky, 2006), 280.

3. Landon Y. Jones, *Great Expectations: America and the Baby Boom Generation* (New York: Coward, McCann and Geoghegan, 1980), 1.

4. Robert May to Charles Widmayer, August 27, 1948, May Papers.

5. Robert May to Charles Widmayer, August 29, 1947, May Papers.

6. Rudolph the Red-Nosed Reindeer, Parker Brothers, circa 1948.

7. Robert May to Charles Widmayer, August 29, 1947, May Papers.

8. Ibid.

9. *Chicago Daily Tribune*, Display ad 101, December 14, 1947, NW3.

10. "3,500,000 Reindeer," *St. Petersburg (FL) Times*, December 21, 1947, 22.

11. Rudolph Push-Out Puzzle Toy, Montgomery Ward, circa 1947.

12. Ibid.

13. Rudolph flashlight, Ward Collection, box 44, folder 3.

14. *Chicago Daily Tribune*, Display ad 116, November 16, 1947, NW4.

15. "Red-Nosed Reindeer!," Gimbels ad, *Milwaukee Journal*, April 5, 1950, Section IIII, page 6.

16. Robert May to Charles Widmayer, August 29, 1947, May Papers.

17. Cross, *Kid's Stuff*, 105.

18. May, "How Rudolph Came to Christmas," 7.

19. "Rudolph the Red-Nosed Reindeer," Maxton Promotional, circa 1947, 11.

20. William Bentley, "Rudolph, the Red Nosed Reindeer," *Chicago Sunday Tribune*, December 17, 1950, 5.

21. "Rudolph the Red-Nosed Reindeer," Maxton Promotional, circa 1947, 11.

22. Robert May to Charles Widmayer, August 29, 1947, May Papers.

23. Lorna Gahagan, "Winking Willie," *Dartmouth Alumni Magazine*, December 1948, 6.

24. Irving S. Heinman Jr. to Robert L. May, January 26, 1940, May Papers.

25. Ibid.

26. Max Fleischer, *Rudolph the Red-Nosed Reindeer*, Jam Handy Organization, 1948.

27. "See the Great Movie of Rudolph the Red-Nosed Reindeer," Montgomery Ward, *Free-Lance Star* (Fredericksburg, VA), December 17, 1948, 3.

28. Ibid.

29. Ibid.

30. Robert May to Charles Widmayer, August 29, 1947, May Papers.

31. "Runaway Rudolph," *Dartmouth Alumni Magazine*, February 1947, 60.

32. "Top Promotion About to Bust for 'Reindeer,'" *Billboard*, December 17, 1949, 39.

33. Robert May to His Children, June 25, 1976, May Papers.

34. Fleischer, *Rudolph*.

35. Ibid.

36. Ibid.

37. William Bentley, "Rudolph, the Red Nosed Reindeer," *Chicago Daily Tribune*, December 17, 1950, 5.

38. Jones, *Great Expectations*, 11.

39. Mintz and Kellogg, *Domestic Revolutions*, 179.

40. Ashby, *With Amusement for All*, 280.

41. Ibid.

42. Ibid., 283.

43. Cross, *Kid's Stuff*, 147.

44. Ibid.

45. William B. Waits, *The Modern Christmas in America: A Cultural History of Gift Giving* (New York: NYU Press, 1993), 192–93.

46. Ashby, *With Amusement for All*, 280.

47. Susan Waggoner, *It's a Wonderful Christmas: The Best of the Holidays, 1940–1965* (New York: Harry N. Abrams, 2004).

48. "Top Promotion About to Bust for 'Reindeer,'" *Billboard*, December 17, 1949, 39.

49. Ibid.

50. "Tale of Rudolph, Only a Reindeer, Brings Fortune," *New York Herald Tribune*, December 19, 1948.

FIVE Johnny Marks, Gene Autry, and
"Rudolph the Red-Nosed Reindeer"

1. Gene Autry, *Back in the Saddle Again* (Garden City, NY: Doubleday, 1978), 28.

2. Ibid.

3. Ibid., 29.

4. Ibid.

5. Ibid.

6. Ibid.

7. Ibid., 30.

8. "'Rudolph' Composer Overnight Hero," *Reading (PA) Eagle*, December 21, 1976, 44.

9. Ibid.

10. Walter Winchell, *Wilmington (DE) News*, December 30, 1949, 4.

11. Barbara Rowes, "Johnny Marks Has Made Millions Off 'Rudolph,' but the Songwriter Still Says Humbug," *People*, December 22, 1980, www.people.com.

12. "Rudolph's Spoor Leads Tunesmiths On," *Dayton Beach (FL) Morning Journal*, December 6, 1958, 8D.

13. William D. Laffler, "Johnny Marks' 'Rudolph' 35 Million Yule Seller," *Schenectady (NY) Gazette*, December 20, 1962, 22.

14. "Rudolph's Spoor Leads Tunesmiths On," 8D.

15. McCandlish Phillips, "Johnny Marks's Rudolph, the Red-Nosed Gold Mine," *New York Times*, December 25, 1969, 39.

16. Holly George-Warren, *Public Cowboy No. 1: The Life and Times of Gene Autry* (New York: Oxford University Press, 2007), 250.

17. Ibid.

18. Ibid.

19. Judy Gail Krasnow, *Rudolph, Frosty, and Captain Kangaroo: The Musical Life of Hecky Krasnow—Producer of the World's Most Beloved Children's Songs* (Santa Monica, CA: Santa Monica Press, 2007), 16.

20. Ibid.

21. Ibid., 19.

22. Ibid., 23.

23. Hal Boyle, "Johnny Marks Hopes to Quit Songs of Yule," *Sarasota (FL) Journal*, December 14, 1956, 23.

24. "Christmas Rock," *Time*, December 12, 1960, 57.

25. Whorf, *American Popular Song Composers*, 137.

26. James Adam Richliano, *Angels We Have Heard: The Christmas Song Stories* (Chatham, NY: Star of Bethlehem Books, 2002), 209.

27. Autry, *Back in the Saddle Again*, 29.

28. Don Cusic, *Gene Autry: His Life and Career* (Jefferson, NC: McFarland, 2010), 127.

six Selling "Rudolph"

1. "Coast Department Stores in All-Out Kidisk Xmas Drives; Supply Plentiful," *Billboard*, November 23, 1946, 18.

2. "Rudolph the Red-Nosed Reindeer: 60th Anniversary," Gene Autry Entertainment, September 12, 2009, www.autry.com.

3. "With Gene Autry and Rodeo, Broadway Is Like Cow Trail," *Reading (PA) Eagle*, October 9, 1949, 32.

4. "Mail Ducats Ready for Mad. Sq. Rodeo," *Billboard*, September 3, 1949, 54.

5. "Autry Gets in Plugs for His Columbia Wax," *Billboard*, October 8, 1949, 4.

6. "Autry's Disks for Kids," *Billboard*, September 24, 1949, 37.

7. "For this year and every year, the fabulous novelty song, 'Rudolph the Red-Nosed Reindeer,'" advertisement, *Billboard*, October 1, 1949, 31.

8. "Songs with Greatest Radio Audiences," *Billboard* (Disk Jockey Supplement), October 22, 1949, 62.

9. "Columbia Preps Large Issue of Christmas Matter on LP," *Billboard*, October 22, 1949, 13.

10. "Children's Records," *Billboard*, November 12, 1949, 28.

11. "Frank Buck for Columbia Kidisks," *Billboard*, November 12, 1949, 17.

12. "Output of Christmas Wax Hits Peak; All Top Artists Pitch for the Santa Claus $$," *Billboard*, December 10, 1949, 1.

13. "Kidiskers Ready for Record Exploitation War in Field,'" *Billboard*, October 14, 1950, 19.

14. "'Rudolph' High on Sheet Sales," *Billboard*, November 11, 1950, 11.

15. Ibid.

16. "Merry Christmas with Gene Autry," *Billboard*, November 25, 1950, 31.

17. "'Rudolph' High on Sheet Sales," *Billboard*, November 11, 1950, 40.

18. Peter Muldavin, *The Complete Guide to Vintage Children's Records: Identification and Value Guide* (Paducah, KY: Collector Books, 2007), 10.

19. Philip Eisenberg and Hecky Krasno, "What Sells Children's Records?," *Saturday Review*, November 27, 1948, 47.

20. Ibid.

21. "Reports Claim Kidisk Boom May Boomerang," *Billboard*, November 23, 1946, 18.

22. "Dark Pre-Yule Picture Fails to Jell as Kidisk Sales Soar," *Billboard*, January 18, 1947, 29.

23. Ibid.

24. Thomas Sugrue, "The Plight before Christmas," *Saturday Review*, November 29, 1947, 49.

25. Bill Simon, "Records for the Young," *Saturday Review*, January 10, 1953, 46.

SEVEN Rudolph's Brand-New Adventures

1. "'Stepmother' Tells All, About Most Famous Reindeer of All," *Milwaukee Journal*, December 16, 1964, part 4, p. 3.

2. "Rudolph Reaches 15," *Chicago Daily Tribune*, A Line o' Type or Two, December 14, 1954, 16.

3. "That Reindeer Is Becoming Tradition," *St. Maurice Valley Chronicle* (Trois Rivières, QC), December 22, 1960, no page.

4. Robert May, *Rudolph's Second Christmas* (RCA, 1951), 17.

5. Bill Seeback, "Grade School Pupils Prepare for Christmas," *Ludington (MI) Daily News*, December 9, 1952, 4.

6. "On the Library Shelves," *Owosso (MI) Argus-Press*, September 28, 1961, section 1, 22.

7. Fredric Wertham, "The Comics . . . Very Funny!," *Saturday Review*, May 29, 1948, 320.

8. Quoted in Ruth A. Inglis, "The Comic Book Problem," *American Mercury*, August 1955, 119.

9. Ashby, *With Amusement for All*, 310.

10. Ibid.

11. Ibid., 311.

12. "Red-Nosed Rudolph to Shine in New Sentinel Comic Strip," *Milwaukee Sentinel*, November 16, 1952, 1.

13. *The Brand-New Adventures of Rudolph the Red-Nosed Reindeer*, DC Comics, 1950, 10.

14. Ibid., 11.

15. *Rudolph the Red-Nosed Reindeer*, King Features Syndicate, 1951.

16. "'Stepmother' Tells All," part 4, p. 3.

17. "Scrapbook Ready for Rudolph Comic," *Deseret News*, November 14, 1957, 12A.

18. James H. Barnett, *The American Christmas: A Study in National Culture* (1954; New York: Arno, 1976), 127.

19. *Dartmouth Alumni Magazine*, April 1958, 42.

EIGHT A New Christmas Tradition

1. "Rudolph Reaches 15."

2. "Rudolph Awarded Niche in Folklore," *Toledo (OH) Blade*, December 23, 1950, 1.

3. Barnett, *American Christmas*, 106.

4. Ibid., 111.

5. Ibid., 111–12.

6. Ibid., 113.

7. Ibid., 114.

8. Richard M. Dorson, "Folklore and Fake Lore," *American Mercury*, March 1950, 335.

9. Ibid., 336.

10. Barnett, *American Christmas*, 24.

11. Stephen Nissenbaum, *The Battle for Christmas: A Cultural History of America's Most Cherished Holiday* (New York: Vintage, 1996), 63.

12. Richard M. Dorson, "Yuletide Gift-Givers," in *The Abbott Christmas Book* (New York: Doubleday, 1960), 63

13. Nissenbaum, *Battle for Christmas*, 64.

14. James B. Twitchell, *Twenty Ads That Shook the World: The Century's Most Groundbreaking Advertising and How It Changed Us All* (New York: Three Rivers, 2000), 104.

15. Ibid., 105.

16. Barnett, *American Christmas*, 26.

17. Eleanor Nangle, "What To Do If Cold Gives Nose a Glow," *Chicago Daily Tribune*, January 2, 1959, A6.

18. Voice of Youth, "A Christmas Letter," *Chicago Tribune*, December 22, 1963, N8.

19. Jean Bond, "Santa's Tailor Sews Suits for Varied Sizes," *Chicago Daily Tribune*, December 15, 1960, N1.

20. "Rudolph with Santa on Hospital Visit," *Los Angeles Examiner*, December 22, 1951.

21. Cindy Dell Clark, *Flights of Fancy, Leaps of Faith: Children's Myths in Contemporary America* (Chicago: University of Chicago Press, 1995), 38–39.

22. "Christmas at Butler Brothers at Lakewood Park . . . Rudolph's Nose Catches on Fire," *Los Angeles Examiner*, December 22, 1951.

23. James T. Carter, "Real Deer with Nose That Glows," *Victoria (TX) Advocate*, December 24, 1961, 3.

24. Ibid.

25. Ibid.

26. Paul Jones, "Rudolph Makes a Hospital Visit," *Hendersonville (NC) Times-News*, January 28, 1984, 9.

27. Ibid.

28. Lucille Younger, "Where's Santa's Rudolph Now? In Skokie, of Course," *Chicago Tribune*, December 25, 1972, 3D.

29. Clark, *Flights of Fancy*, 104–5.

30. "The Package Parade," *Nashua (NH) Cavalier*, July 1950, 7.

NINE Rankin/Bass's *Rudolph*

1. Tim Hollis, *Christmas Wishes: A Catalog of Vintage Holiday Treats and Treasures*. Mechanicsburg, PA: Stackpole Books, 2010, 42.

2. Ibid., 43.

3. Robert May, *Rudolph's Second Christmas*, RCA, 1951.

4. Harvey Pack, "NBC Christmas Special: Burl Ives Narrates NBC Christmas Special," *Meriden Journal*, December 5, 1964, A1.

5. "GE's Animagic Animal Act," *Sponsor*, September 4, 1964, 46.

6. Ibid.

7. Ibid., 48.

8. Ibid.

9. Ibid.

10. Ibid.

11. Ibid.

12. "Rudolph, at 16, Still Sleighs 'Em," *Billboard*, September 19, 1964, 6.

13. "GE's Animagic Animal Act," 47.

14. Ibid.

TEN An American Hero

1. Eileen Ogintz, "Afterglow: The Man Who Created Rudolph from an Idea That Almost Didn't Fly," *Chicago Tribune*, December 13, 1990, C19.

2. Ibid.

3. Bob Hugel, "Rudolph's Nose Still Shining Bright 50 Years Later," *Rutland (VT) Daily Herald*, December 18, 1989, 9.

4. "Rudolph All Red-Nosed Over Stamp of Approval," USPS, November 6, 2014, http://about.usps.com.

5. Richard Goleszowski, *Hooves of Fire*, BBC, 1999.

6. Corky Quakenbush, "Raging Rudolph," *MADtv*, December 16, 1995.

7. Ibid.

8. Ibid.

9. Chel White, "The Narrator That Ruined Christmas," *Saturday Night Live*, December 15, 2001.

10. Ibid.

11. Ibid.

12. Ibid.

13. Aflac, Rudolph Commercial, 2007.

14. Ibid.

15. Bob Garfield, "It Takes a True Ad Critic to See Where Aflac Spot Went Wrong," *Ad Age*, November 26, 2007, www.adage.com.

16. AT&T, Island of Misfit Toys commercial, 2009.

17. Ibid.

18. Fred Davis, *Yearning for Yesterday: A Sociology of Nostalgia* (New York: Free Press, 1979), 118.

19. Ibid., 122.

20. Ibid., 126.

bibliography

Archival Collections

Stanley Frankel. Papers. Northwestern University Library, Evanston, IL.

Robert L. May. Papers. Rauner Special Collections Library, Dartmouth College, Hanover, NH.

Montgomery Ward Collection. American Heritage Center, University of Wyoming, Laramie.

Books, Periodicals, Other Media

Aflac. Rudolph commercial. 2007.

Ashby, LeRoy. *With Amusement for All: A History of American Popular Culture since 1830*. Lexington: University Press of Kentucky, 2006.

AT&T. Island of Misfit Toys commercial. 2009.

Autry, Gene, with Mickey Herskowitz. *Back in the Saddle Again*. Garden City, NY: Doubleday, 1978.

Barnett, James H. *The American Christmas: A Study in National Culture*. New York: Arno, 1976 (reprint edition). First published by Macmillan, 1954.

Belk, Russell W. "A Child's Christmas in America: Santa Claus as Deity, Consumption as Religion." *Journal of American Culture* 10, no. 1 (Spring 1987): 87–100.

Bentley, William. "Rudolph, the Red Nosed Reindeer." *Chicago Sunday Tribune*, December 17, 1950.

Bloom, Nate. "Shining a Light on the Largely Untold Story of the Origins of Rudolph, the Red-Nosed Reindeer." *Interfaith Family*, December 20, 2011. www .interfaithfamily.com.

Bond, Jean. "Santa's Tailor Sews Suits for Varied Sizes." *Chicago Daily Tribune*, December 15, 1960.

Bowler, Gerry. *The World Encyclopedia of Christmas*. Toronto: McClelland and Stewart, 2000.

Boyle, Hal. "Johnny Marks Hopes to Quit Songs of Yule." *Sarasota (FL) Journal*, December 14, 1956

Caldwell, Wilber W. *Cynicism and the Evolution of the American Dream*. Dulles, VA: Potomac, 2006.

Carter, James T. "Real Deer with Nose That Glows." *Victoria (TX) Advocate*, December 24, 1961.

Charles, Barbara Fahs, and J. R. Taylor. *Dream of Santa: Haddon Sundblom's Vision*. Alexandria, VA: Staples and Charles, 1992.

Chicago Daily Tribune. Display ad 101. December 14, 1947.

———. Display ad 116. November 16, 1947.

———. "Rudolph Reaches 15." A Line o' Type or Two. December 14, 1954.

Chicago Tribune. "A Christmas Letter." Voice of Youth. December 22, 1963.

Clark, Cindy Dell. *Flights of Fancy, Leaps of Faith: Children's Myths in Contemporary America*. Chicago: University of Chicago Press, 1995.

Coca-Cola Collectible Santas. Dallas: Beckett, 2000.

Cohen, Lizabeth. *A Consumers' Republic: The Politics of Mass Consumption in Postwar America*. New York: Vintage, 2004.

Collins, Ace. *Stories behind the Best-Loved Songs of Christmas*. Grand Rapids, MI: Zondervan, 2001.

Connelly, Mark, ed. *Christmas at the Movies: Images of Christmas in American, British and European Cinema*. New York: I. B. Tauris, 2000.

Coontz, Stephanie. *The Way We Never Were: American Families and the Nostalgia Trap*. New York: Basic Books, 1992.

Cross, Gary S. *An All-Consuming Century: Why Commercialism Won in Modern America*. New York: Columbia University Press, 2000.

———. *The Cute and the Cool: Wondrous Innocence and Modern American Children's Culture*. New York: Oxford University Press, 2004.

———. *Kids' Stuff: Toys and the Changing World of American Childhood*. Cambridge, MA: Harvard University Press, 1997.

Cusic, Don. *Gene Autry: His Life and Career*. Jefferson, NC: McFarland, 2007.

Dartmouth Alumni Magazine. "Runaway Rudolph." February 1947.

Davis, Fred. *Yearning for Yesterday: A Sociology of Nostalgia*. New York: Free Press, 1979.

Daytona Beach (FL) Morning Journal. "Rudolph's Spoor Leads Tunesmiths On." December 6, 1958.

DC Comics. *The Brand-New Adventures of Rudolph the Red-Nosed Reindeer*. 1950–62.

deChant, Dell. *The Sacred Santa: Religious Dimensions of Consumer Culture*. Eugene, OR: Wipf and Stock, 2002.

Deseret News (Salt Lake City). "Scrapbook Ready for Rudolph Comic." November 14, 1957.

Dickens, Charles. *A Christmas Carol*. New York: Dover, 1991. First published by Chapman and Hall, London, 1843.

Dorson, Richard M. "Folklore and Fake Lore." *American Mercury*, March 1950.

———. "Yuletide Gift-Givers." Reprinted in *The Abbott Christmas Book*, 63–66. Garden City, NJ: Doubleday, 1960.

Dundes, Alan. *Christmas as a Reflection of American Culture*. Privately printed, 1970.

Eisenberg, Philip, and Hecky Krasno. "What Sells Children's Records?" *Saturday Review*, November 27, 1948.

Evans, G. S. "Consumerism in the USA: A Nation of Junkies?" *Synthesis/Regeneration* 57 (Winter 2012): 23–26.

Fleischer, Max. *Rudolph the Red-Nosed Reindeer*. Jam Handy Organization, 1948.

Forbes, Bruce David. *Christmas: A Candid History*. Berkeley: University of California Press, 2007.

Foster, Inez Whiteley. "Red-Nosed Reindeer: Rudolph Finds Way to Little People's Hearts through Robert May." *Christian Science Monitor*, December 4, 1948.

Free-Lance Star (Fredericksburg, VA). "See the Great Movie of Rudolph the Red-Nosed Reindeer" (Montgomery Ward ad). December 17, 1948.

Gahagan, Lorna. "Winking Willie." *Dartmouth Alumni Magazine*, December 1948.

Gardner, Martin. *The Annotated "Night before Christmas": A Collection of Sequels, Parodies, and Imitations of Clement Moore's Immortal Ballad about Santa Claus*. New York: Simon and Schuster, 1991.

Garfield, Bob. "It Takes a True Ad Critic to See Where Aflac Spot Went Wrong." *Ad Age*, November 26, 2007. www.adage.com.

Gene Autry Entertainment. "Rudolph the Red-Nosed Reindeer: 60th Anniversary." September 12, 2009. www.autry.com.

George-Warren, Holly. *Public Cowboy No. 1: The Life and Times of Gene Autry*. New York: Oxford University Press, 2007.

Goleszowski, Richard. *Hooves of Fire*. Animated television special. BBC, 1999.

Hallowell, Billy. "Do You Know the Real History of 'Rudolph the Red-Nosed Reindeer?'" *Blaze*, December 24, 2011. www.theblaze.com.

Hirschman, Elizabeth C., ed. *Interpretive Consumer Research*. Provo, UT: Association for Consumer Research, 1989.

Hoge, Cecil C., Sr. *The First Hundred Years Are the Toughest: What We Can Learn from the Century of Competition between Sears and Wards*. Berkeley, CA: Ten Speed, 1988.

Hollis, Tim. *Christmas Wishes: A Catalog of Vintage Holiday Treats and Treasures*. Mechanicsburg, PA: Stackpole, 2010.

Horsley, Richard, and James Tracy, eds. *Christmas Unwrapped: Consumerism, Christ, and Culture*. Harrisburg, PA: Trinity Press International, 2001.

Hugel, Bob. "Rudolph's Nose Still Shining Bright 50 Years Later." *Rutland (VT) Daily Herald*, December 18, 1989.

I'll Be Home for Christmas: The Library of Congress Revisits the Spirit of Christmas during World War II. New York: Delacorte Press, 1999.

Inglis, Ruth A. "The Comic Book Problem." *American Mercury*, August 1955.

Jones, Landon Y. *Great Expectations: America and the Baby Boom Generation*. New York: Coward, McCann and Geoghegan, 1980.

Jones, Paul. "Rudolph Makes a Hospital Visit." *Hendersonville (NC) Times-News*, January 28, 1984.

Krasnow, Judy Gail. *Rudolph, Frosty, and Captain Kangaroo: The Musical Life of Hecky Krasnow—Producer of the World's Most Beloved Children's Songs*. Santa Monica, CA: Santa Monica Press, 2007.

Lewis, Tiffany J. "Rudolph Goes Down in History." *Premier*, December 1994.

Liston, Jim. "Rudolph the Red-Nosed Reindeer Took Him for a Ride." *Today's Health*, December 1959.

Los Angeles Examiner. "Christmas at Butler Brothers at Lakewood Park . . . Rudolph's Nose Catches on Fire." December 22, 1951.

——— ."Rudolph with Santa on Hospital Visit." December 22, 1951.

Major, Ralph H., and Stanley Frankel. "Rudolph That Amazing Reindeer." *Coronet*, December 1948.

Marling, Karla Ann. *Merry Christmas! Celebrating America's Greatest Holiday*. Cambridge, MA: Harvard University Press, 2000.

Marsh, Dave, and Steve Propes. *Merry Christmas, Baby: Holiday Music from Bing to Sting*. New York: Little, Brown, 1993.

Maxton Promotional. "Rudolph the Red-Nosed Reindeer." Circa 1947.

May, Robert, L. "How Rudolph Came to Christmas." *Syracuse (NY) Herald-Journal*, December 22, 1963.

———. "Rudolph and I Were Something Alike." *Guideposts*, January 1975.

———. *Rudolph Shines Again*. Maxton, 1954.

———. *Rudolph's Second Christmas*. RCA, 1951.

———. *Rudolph the Red-Nosed Reindeer*. Carlisle, MA: Applewood, reprint, 1990.

McGovern, Charles F. *Sold American: Consumption and Citizenship, 1890–1945*. Chapel Hill: University of North Carolina Press, 2006.

McLuhan, Marshall. *The Mechanical Bride*. New York: Vanguard, 1951.

Mendelson, Lee, with Bill Melendez. *A Charlie Brown Christmas: The Making of a Tradition*. New York: Harper Resource, 2000.

Menendez, Albert J., and Shirley C. Menendez. *Christmas Songs Made in America: Favorite Holiday Melodies and the Stories of Their Origins*. Nashville: Cumberland House, 1999.

Miller, Daniel, ed. *Unwrapping Christmas*. New York: Oxford University Press, 1993.

Milwaukee Journal. "'Stepmother' Tells All, About Most Famous Reindeer of All." December 16, 1964.

———. "Red-Nosed Reindeer!" Gimbels ad. April 5, 1950.

Milwaukee Sentinel. "Red-Nosed Rudolph to Shine in New Sentinel Comic Strip." November 16, 1952.

Mintz, Steven, and Susan Kellog. *Domestic Revolutions: A Social History of American Family Life*. New York: Free Press, 1987.

Muldavin, Peter. *The Complete Guide to Vintage Children's Records Identification and Value Guide*. Paducah, KY: Collector Books, 2007.

Nashua (NH) Cavalier. "The Package Parade." July 1950.

Newsweek. "Rudolph Was Almost Rollo." December 7, 1964.

New York Herald Tribune. "Tale of Rudolph, Only a Reindeer, Brings Fortune." December 19, 1948.

Nissenbaum, Stephen. *The Battle for Christmas: A Cultural History of America's Most Cherished Holiday*. New York: Vintage, 1996.

Ogintz, Eileen. "Afterglow: The Man Who Created Rudolph from an Idea That Almost Didn't Fly." *Chicago Tribune*, December 13, 1990.

Otfinoski, Steve. *The Golden Age of Novelty Songs*. New York: Billboard, 2000.

Owosso (MI) Argus-Press. "On the Library Shelves." September 28, 1961.

Pack, Harvey. "NBC Christmas Special: Burl Ives Narrates NBC Christmas Special." *Meriden (CT) Journal*, December 5, 1964.

Phillips, McCandlish. "Johnny Marks's Rudolph, the Red-Nosed Gold Mine." *New York Times*, December 25, 1969.

Pleck, Elizabeth H. *Celebrating the Family: Ethnicity, Consumer Culture, and Family Rituals*. Cambridge, MA: Harvard University Press, 2000.

Pupovac, Jessica. "Writing 'Rudolph': The Original Red-Nosed Manuscript." *National Public Radio*, December 25, 2013. www.npr.org.

Quakenbush, Corky. "Raging Rudolph." *MADtv*, 1995.

Reading (PA) Eagle. "'Rudolph' Composer Overnight Hero." December 21, 1976.

———. "With Gene Autry and Rodeo, Broadway Is Like Cow Trail." October 9, 1949.

Restad, Penne L. *Christmas in America: A History*. New York: Oxford University Press, 1995.

Richliano, James Adam. *Angels We Have Heard: The Christmas Song Stories*. Chatham, NY: Star of Bethlehem Books, 2002.

Roosevelt, Franklin D. "Statement on the Seizure of Montgomery Ward Co. Properties." December 27, 1944. www.presidency.ucsb.edu.

Rosen, Jody. *White Christmas: The Story of an American Song*. New York: Scribner, 2002.

Rowes, Barbara. "Johnny Marks Has Made Millions off 'Rudolph,' but the Songwriter Still Says Humbug." *People*, December 22, 1980. www.people.com.

Schmidt, Leigh Eric. *Consumer Rites: The Buying and Selling of American Holidays*. Princeton, NJ: Princeton University Press, 1995.

Seeback, Bill. "Grade School Pupils Prepare for Christmas." *Ludington (MI) Daily News*, December 9, 1952.

Simon, Bill. "Records for the Young." *Saturday Review*, January 10, 1953.

Smith, Jacob. *Spoken Word: Postwar American Phonograph Cultures*. Los Angeles: University of California Press, 2011.

Smith, Tilly. *The Real Rudolph: A Natural History of the Reindeer*. Gloucestershire, UK: Sutton, 2006.

Sponsor. "GE's Animagic Animal Act." September 4, 1964.

St. Maurice Valley Chronicle (Trois-Rivières, QC). "That Reindeer Is Becoming Tradition." December 22, 1960.

St. Petersburg (FL) Times. "3,500,000 Reindeer." December 21, 1947.

Sugrue, Thomas. "The Plight before Christmas." *Saturday Review*, November 29, 1947.

Time. "Christmas Rock." December 12, 1960.

Twitchell, James B. *Adcult USA: The Triumph of Advertising in American Culture.* New York: Columbia University Press, 1996.

———. *Twenty Ads That Shook the World: The Century's Most Groundbreaking Advertising and How It Changed Us All.* New York: Three Rivers, 2000.

USPS (United States Postal Service). "Rudolph All Red-Nosed Over Stamp of Approval." November 6, 2014. http://about.usps.com.

Waggoner, Susan. *It's a Wonderful Christmas: The Best of the Holidays, 1940–1965.* New York: Stewart, Tabori and Chang, 2004.

Waits, William B. *The Modern Christmas in America: A Cultural History of Gift Giving.* New York: NYU Press, 1993.

Washburn, Michael. "Boca Once Was Home to Rudolph's Creator." *Boca Raton (FL) News,* December 14, 1990.

Washington Times. "'Jingle Bells' Dispute Jangles On." December 24, 2003. www. washingtontimes.com.

Wertham, Fredric. "The Comics . . . Very Funny!" *Saturday Review*, May 29, 1948.

Whitburn, Joel. *Christmas in the Charts: 1920–2004.* New York: Billboard, 2004.

White, Chel. "The Narrator That Ruined Christmas." *Saturday Night Live*, December 15, 2001.

Whiteley, Shelia, ed. *Christmas, Ideology and Popular Culture.* Edinburgh: Edinburgh University Press, 2008.

Whorf, Michael. *American Popular Song Composers: Oral Histories, 1920s–1950s.* Jefferson, NC: McFarland, 2012.

Winchell, Walter. *Wilmington (DE) News*, December 30, 1949.

Younger, Lucille. "Where's Santa's Rudolph Now? In Skokie, of Course." *Chicago Tribune*, December 25, 1972.

Zielinski, Stan. "Rudolph the Red-Nosed Reindeer." *Children's Picturebook Collecting*, November 2, 2008. www.1stedition.net.

index

Note: Page numbers in *italics* indicate illustrations